The Sell

Set Yourself Up for a Lifetime of Selling Success

**"Don't Give Up
Before you Make It
To the Top"**

Antonio Clyde Smith

The Sellionaire™
Published by Hudson Dockett Publishing, Inc

©2008 by Antonio Clyde Smith
International Standard Book Number:978-0-615-22530-2

Cover Design by Bill Spiers
Printed in the U.S.A.

Library of Congress Cataloging –in-Publication Data

Distributed by Hudson Dockett Publishing, Inc.

For Information:
Antonio Clyde Smith International
925 Main St. Ste 50-71
Stone Mountain, Ga 30083
678-476-3715
770-234-5849 fax
www.thesellionaire.com

Sign up for FREE weekly e-zine
info@thesellionaire.com

Dedication

This Book is dedicated to two of the best salespeople I know - my daughter Taylor and my son Tyler Smith.

Dear Creator -

"*Please let this book reach all those that it was intended to inspire. Let the things that I've done be a testimony that helps someone achieve the results that they desire. Continue to give me wisdom, Lord, for I am only a vessel that you have given an opportunity to use to spread this message. May all who read this book have great success in their lives and be inspired by the trials and errors that I've made on my sales journey. This is the best industry I've ever been in that rewards you for hard work and self-application.*"

You'd better hope your competition doesn't have this book, because you're about to learn valuable secrets to making more money by closing more sales! This action-packed book will help you unleash your inner competitive spirit. You'll learn how top salesmen close more sales through the new techniques that work in today's marketplace. No other book will show you how to start imagining and start earning faster than this one.

If you have something to sell, you can have it sold within 30 days after you read this book, no matter what it is! The techniques I'm going to show you here have been tried and tested. Whether you are new to sales or a seasoned veteran, you will learn how to add to your arsenal of deals CLOSED. Go ahead - write down your goals and get ready to go, because you'll be motivated to reach them all this year. No more waiting on the New Year to roll in before you get started!

This book will help you put procrastination aside and go after your goals with a vengeance. In the following chapters, you'll see the true value in yourself to ignite the fire to live out your dreams and your true potential. You'll light the fire you need to keep going and never give up. You'll learn why you must be successful, no matter what. You'll learn how to create a sales plan beyond your ordinary reach, grow your company through international markets, and reach customers even if you don't speak their language. Let me help you make this year different from last year step by step. Get ready to indulge yourself in the dreams you were born for. Let's walk into your new reality today!

My Story -

I grew up in a single-parent home in Valdosta, Georgia; a small town near the Georgia-Florida state line. I was raised in great part by my godmother who instilled great spirituality in my life. Every Sunday we went to church - rain or shine. Sometimes we went every day of the week.

Even though we were very poor, my godmother was rich in love and happiness. She took good care of the little that she did have and made the most out of every situation. She was a true survivor who was proactive. She was a care-giver in the church, and everyone loved her. We didn't have cable TV or central air in the house. If we were hot we just went outside and sat in the old rocking chair on the porch.

Everything seemed so simple then. The people in the church raised money for my godmother from time to time because she had financial difficulties trying to raise me and her own kids as a single parent. We wore clothes that were given to us as hand-me-downs. Sometimes my god-brother Willie and I would pick up cans so we could afford food for dinner. Willie was a tall man my godmother had taken in as a child after his own mother abandoned him. He never complained about anything and helped her care for me until I was five years old.

One day my real mother decided to move to Atlanta and took me with her. I was so attached to my dear godmother that I cried every night to see her again. I was so far from the home I had grown used to and even though we were poor, the values she taught me lasted a lifetime.

My real mother was a single parent herself and had six kids in addition to me. She hoped she'd find better opportunities in Atlanta. Once we got there, the man that had come with her left her and she had to take care of all seven of us of on her own. She was new to the city and desperate to put a roof over our heads. Through government assistance, we eventually moved into a brick building with brick walls and concrete floors – what now would be called the "projects" or the ghetto.

I was ten years old when we moved to Atlanta. Since I was the oldest of the seven kids, it was up to me to watch the other children while my mother worked odd jobs. Several times we almost wound up in foster care when our mother left home for days at a time. People would realize we were alone and would call the child protection agencies. I remember many nights sitting on the iron stairs inside our apartment wishing I had never been born into such a family. I asked God why I had to live this way. I cried many nights longing to be in the home I knew back in Valdosta. I'm sure my godmother cried too as she looked at the stars praying for me and I looked out the window wishing I was there. This was my new life as I knew it and I couldn't do anything other than adapt as best as I could.

Almost every day there were fights in the projects. Many of the kids in my class joined gangs and some lost their lives. Every day when I got off the bus to go to school, I'd see drug dealers and users lining the streets. These conditions had a huge effect on a lot of the kids I knew. Many of them acted out in violence or intimidation. Others bought guns simply to protect themselves. Often I would think that this was no way to live. But somehow in the middle of poverty I still dreamed of a better life.

Back in Valdosta, the one TV channel my godmother got without cable showed the program, "Lifestyles of the Rich and Famous." The host, Robin Leach, would interview celebrities and showcase their lifestyles. The people on that show were a far cry from where I was, but I dreamed of being like them. I was too young to get a job and no one would hire me because of child labor laws, but I managed to find things to do that put a few dollars in my pocket from time to time. I worked at different odd jobs from dishwashing to carrying bags for a shopper to pumping gas. When I was sixteen, I managed to get a work permit which allowed me to work for newspaper company processing inserts. Later I started scalping tickets at Turner Hill Stadium and parking cars to make money.

I desperately wanted the better life that seemed so far out of reach to everyone around me. It seemed like everyone just gave up and accepted the card life had dealt them. I began to skip classes in school because I couldn't concentrate on my homework while caring for my sisters and brothers. I needed to make money to get what I needed. My mom bought me shoes once and to me they were beautiful. They were blue and white and on the first day of school I thought I was the freshest thing in the class. But the other kids laughed at my new shoes because they weren't name branded. I just wanted to make myself invisible. Here I was feeling good about myself and the kids from my own neighborhood were mocking me because I didn't have the latest shoes on the first day of school? I thought my new shoes were a step up from the pink shoes I had worn before I got them!

Eventually, I realized that if I wanted to get something done I'd have to make it happen on my own. With seven mouths to feed, even buying shoes for me was difficult for my mom. We lived near the Atlanta Stadium and from time to time I would walk to the stadium to resell tickets. I was inspired by Ted Turner who owned the stadium. I would read about Turner and how he had a huge vested interest in not only the stadium, but the baseball team itself!

One day I found an ad in the newspaper that said I could earn five hundred or more dollars a week. If I could earn that much, I thought, I'd be able to pay for my own shoes and help my mother more. I went in for an interview, but when the manager saw me, he told me that I was too young for the position and to come back when I turned 18.

I was crushed. Just when I found a way to earn some serious money I was turned away. I didn't know what to do next. As I turned away, a heavy set guy walked in. He had heard everything. He looked at me and said, "Let's see what we can do." I was so excited to have an opportunity, but soon I realized that there was a new challenge waiting for me. I was going to have to learn how to sell a product over the phone.

The product I was selling was house wares – knives, pots and pans. All the sales were by phone. I was the youngest person on the sales team and I had no idea how to sell. For the first two weeks I had no success on the phone. I thought I'd never reach the results of $500 to $1000 a week the

ad had proclaimed. One night I thought about it as I lay in the bed. I thought, "I don't have a choice. I have to make this work."
I spent hours learning more about the product. I would sit next to the heavy hitters who were earning the income I wanted and made a serious commitment to make it work. Before long, I became the new heavy hitter on the block. I was now challenging the big dogs daily. I began to help my mother more. As soon as I was able to drive, I bought my own car.

I found out the hard way that you can learn how to sell and that if you keep learning you will sell well. Eventually, I was offered a job at a major bank in their card division. I was their top salesman for several years. My first successes led to more and more successes but also some failures along the way . I had to start several of my own companies before I was successful in one of them. Through trial and error, I learned from each failure and actually became more successful because I learned what not to do.

Since those early days, I've sold thousands of products and services and made millions of dollars in annual residual sales for the companies I've work for. I've learned that no matter what your product is, you must know how to effectively sell. You are either in sales or in sales support. Sales are the lifeline of the American economy. Millions of people get up every morning and hit the challenging streets to market products and services. This book is designed to show you how you can get the competitive edge for tremendous success through hard work and true salesmanship.

Table of Contents

Introduction –The Opportunity to Sell

Sales was the dynamic force that helped me change my life. It gave me the financial resources to travel, to purchase the car of my dreams, and to reach my goals. The important thing about sales is that no matter what your background or ethnicity, it all comes down to your skills. You don't have to graduate at the top of your class or even need to go to school to earn more money. You simply have to learn how to effectively convey your product to the market. If the marketplace and if the product has appeal and satisfies a need, you've won half the battle.

The great thing about sales is that there's no limit to the income you can earn. You can make more than a lawyer or doctor. You can travel around the world or send your kids to private schools. If you live in America you are blessed because you're living in a country that believes in capitalism. I believe that everyone should strive to be a part of the real American dream.

Your Biggest Year Ever!

It's your turn now. You've helped movie stars make the biggest weekend box office hit in history. You've helped the companies on the New York Stock Exchange make billions of dollars. You've prayed for this moment all your life. Now is the time to make it happen. You said you wanted to make things happen this year; let's make it happen now! It's time to prove to yourself that you can make your dreams come true.

We often camouflage our problems by deciding to do the right thing but then failing to follow through. The true test is in working hard to get the results that you desire. Tell yourself that you will finish the race on top. You have no other choice but to win. You are a champion who was born to succeed. The time to start is NOW. This week, instead of spending your whole check on video games, why not make an investment in personal education that will help you go down the right path. When you're driving between appointments, stock your car's CD player with motivational material that helps you stay focused on your goals.

Sure, it's a challenge to reach your goals these days. If it were easy, everyone would do it and we couldn't call it success any more - we'd have to call it something else!

Recently, I made up my mind to learn how to skate. I had seen how much fun skaters were having, and I made up my mind to learn. I followed up on my decision by purchasing a pair of skates and protective gear. I fell several times in the beginning weeks. Then I sprained my wrist, which put me out for about a week. But I didn't give up. I thought, "If I stop now I'll never see what it feels like to enjoy those skates." Inside I wanted to quit but I didn't let doubt set in. When I was back on my feet, I went back to the hill where I had fallen. As I turned the curve and saw the hill, my mind flashed back to my fall. But I told myself, "I'm going to win this time!"

I confidently honed in on the curve and concentrated as I took the turn. Somewhere in that turn I became a true skater. As I faced my fear, the doubt faded away. Now I skate with more confidence and enjoy the sport more than ever.

You see, only fear is holding you back from your victory! You must look fear and doubt in the eye with a mean face and tell yourself that you are going to win! Speak to that doubting voice. "You said I couldn't do it, but I will. You said I'd give up but I didn't. You didn't believe in me, but I believed in myself."

Go after the promise you were chosen to go after right now. Your life will start to improve immediately. Before you know it, you will become the person that others look to for answers. There will be no doubt that you can make things happen. Let's make this your best year ever. Your success is a process, not a competition.

Ray Croc, the founder of McDonald's, founded his legacy at the age of 55. There are people in their 80s who go back to school to get the diploma they've always dreamed of. You can start now by doing little things day by day to get you to your ultimate dreams. This is a process you <u>must</u> start, you don't have time to waste.

Start today and make a list of all the things you want to accomplish within the next five years. You can start a whole new chapter in your life right now. This time next year you could be doing a job you love and driving the car of your dreams.

It all starts right now. It's time to stop daydreaming and start believing. Step by step you will work it. Push up by push up you'll reach your goals. There will be sunny days when you'll think "I just want to have fun today and work tomorrow," but that's the voice that you must fear the most. As soon as you hear that voice, that's the time to make up your mind to do what you're supposed to do. Don't put it off for the next day. This is the kind of thinking that will get you moving toward your dreams and ahead of the competition.

There will be rainy days that are wet and cold, but to succeed, you must continue to move forward - no matter what. Use the vision of your future goals right now to get you through the challenging time of the present. God gave you the power to visualize your dreams. He said you can call those things that are not as if they are. <u>You</u> are the missing piece of the puzzle. <u>You</u> and only you will determine whether or not you reach your ultimate goals.

You Must Be Crazy!

Ideas can be funny things when they are presented to people who aren't quite ready for them. They can inspire people to do great and wonderful things that they might not otherwise have even thought of doing. Or they can bring out the worst in humanity. The dark little underside of stagnancy that everyone believed was well hidden. If you are an innovator or an idea person, you know exactly the kind of resistance to change I'm talking about.

When people are stuck in a rut and they can't even see it, sometimes it takes a special kind of person to wake them up to their reality. Before you go jumping in to fill such a revered position, keep in mind that when you do, you're going to meet up with some serious resistance.

In the mid twentieth century, there was a man who did his absolute best to bring positive change to the world. He was laughed at. He was ridiculed by his own people. He was beaten many times. He was arrested more than twenty times. Eventually, he was killed. His name was Dr. Martin Luther King, Jr. and many people believed he was driven beyond reason.

Can you picture yourself in the world that Dr. King was trying to change? Perhaps you were there, or you know someone who was. If you were there in that time and you found yourself in a similar situation today, would you do anything differently? Would you choose Dr. King's method of peaceful resistance or perhaps take a more direct approach as many of his rivals did? Would you be willing to pay the price that he so readily accepted to bring about the change that you seek?

Thankfully, most of us aren't forced to make such dangerous decisions in today's world. Sure, people will probably always be resistant to change, but at the very least we can say that the stakes are a bit lower. We can talk about new things and many people will at least consider them before telling us to get lost. But it still takes a different sort of determination to keep on trying until the change that you seek becomes a greater reality.

So what's your idea that you can't wait to sell? A new kind of car, perhaps, or a cell phone that massages your aching head while you work? These types of changes might seem insignificant when compared to those that Dr. King helped to bring about, but they still can revolutionize the way people walk, talk, think, and act.

There will always be stronger people who would like nothing more than for you to disappear so that they can go about their normal business as though you hadn't just made their livelihood obsolete. They'll make you feel guilty about the jobs you are taking away from good American people. They'll tell you that people like you will be the downfall of our truly great society. They'll say you must be crazy. When you hear these

things, remember that they've all been said before. They have been said to people like Dr. Martin Luther King, Jr., and to Henry Ford, and to countless other dreamers who saw a better way for people to live.
If we were all as strongly driven as the great people I've mentioned here, just imagine what the world might be like! The problems that could have been solved. The sheer power of people acting together for one good purpose. If we make the choice to become so driven, there is nothing of this world that can hinder our efforts so long as they are guided by the conscience that we all have been given. When we think of the struggles of the great men and women who came before us, we can be glad that they accomplished the most difficult tasks that would otherwise have prevented us from living as we do. But above all, we must not become complacent with that knowledge.

We must all be the great innovators of our day, or else risk the stagnation of our world once again and the destruction of all those great works. We must all be driven beyond reason because it is only then that we know we are on the right path.

When you dream big and go after your goals, you can expect to be called crazy. That's a good thing! Let me explain. Martin Luther King was called crazy. In the Deep South where because of the color of his skin he had to sit in the back of the bus he had to have a dream that one day things could change! The Wright Brothers were called crazy; everyone knew it was impossible for men to fly! They kept on going in spite of their critics and now millions of people fly on a daily basis.

What is a Sellionaire?

The key to your success is to become what I call a "Sellionaire." This is the unique individual whose determination wins out in the end. When others say to call it quits, the Sellionaire keeps on going. The Sellionaire is the master of his or her circumstances. The Sellionaire uses adversity to fuel his future successes.

If you're a real Sellionaire, you'll have some key characteristics:

A Sellionaire always has a way to write things down. He is always ready to seize an opportunity or write down an idea that inspires him/her to do something big. Ideas can come at any time, in any place. The Sellionaire knows how to capture the ideas and make them a reality.
A Sellionaire is a leader in his/her field, but is never afraid to ask questions that will increase his/her chances of success.
A Sellionaire is always proactive in dealing with a challenge.
A Sellionaire invests in education that keeps him/her focused on reaching his/her goals.
A Sellionaire never uses the words 'broke' or 'can't' because he knows that's the type of language poor people use. A Sellionnaire says 'I Can' and 'I Will''.
A Sellionaire sets big goals that pushes his or her boundaries.
A Sellionare expects obstacles to come up and prepares for them on a daily basis.
A Sellionaire knows how to turn a negative situation into a positive.
A Sellionaire <u>never</u> quits.
A Sellionaire creates his/her own reality.

Dare to dream again – A Parable

There once was a man who dreamed of building a castle.
Although he was a carpenter by trade and made little income,
He had a dream one night that he would live in a castle.
So the next day he told a friend about this dream he had.
His friend laughed and said, "You're not smart enough to build a castle -
You never went to school!"
The man walked away, thinking to himself "Well, maybe I'm not smart
enough to build a castle."
But the next night he had the same dream.
He was so excited, he went out and told another friend who was a street
merchant.
That friend said, "You'll never be able to build a castle! That would take a
lot of money."
The man once again walked away thinking to himself "I don't really have
enough money to build a castle," and went on with his day.
But the third night, the man had the same dream. This time he saw
himself inside his castle. The next day he rushed out and told his neighbor
who was a shield maker.
His neighbor said, "You can't own a castle. That's only reserved for
important people. You're only a carpenter."
The man strolled toward the city wondering why he had been having these
dreams because they seemed so real each night.
As he was walking to the city as he usually did each morning, he had an
idea.
He raced back home, pulling his donkey and load as fast as he could.
Once at home, he opened a chest that contained dusty papers with notes
he had written down.
It was an idea he had written down several years ago.
His idea was to build a pipeline that would bring water to all the villages
throughout the city.
The idea had come to him one night while lying under the moon on a calm
night.
The land where he lived had been given to him when his father passed on.

The land was right on the edge of a stream that ran into a well on the property.

There was an endless supply of water in the well.

The man decided to start building the pipeline little by little.

He hired laborers to work for him in exchange for food.

One day the pipeline was complete and it was a success!

The pipeline brought water to all the villages in the area.

The man charged a nickel for a bucket of water to each of the huts in the village.

In a short time, the man became rich and bought the castle that he dreamed of and lived happily ever after.

You see, your dreams are only the end results of a puzzle that you must put together. They are reached by simple steps taken each day over time. By taking action you will reach your dreams. Your capital may not be money, but a mind made up to use what you have now to reach them.

- Antonio Smith

Chapter 1 – Time Management

> *"The bad news is: Time flies.*
> *The good news is: You're the pilot."*
> - Michael Altshuler

To achieve success, you must know how to manage your time. You must be able to delegate your time to the right task. Some people are very busy, but they are busy doing the wrong things at the wrong time. They never seem to have enough time for the important things. I've seen sales people miss big commissions because they are simply not in the right place at the right time.

Never waste your prime time hours doing miniscule tasks. Keep yourself focused 100% on your prospects. For example, if you market products to businesses, your primetime is probably 9 to 5 when they are open. Don't take care of your errands or sit around daydreaming during those hours! You should be out in front of new prospects.

Time management is really no mystery. It doesn't require intense thinking or research to understand. What is much more important is how much those time management principles and techniques become a part of you, how deeply they penetrate into your mind. This is why learning in small bits over an extended period of time, with each of those bits repeated a few times, will beat the effect of any intense time management seminar.

With good time management skills you are in control of your time and your life, of your stress and energy levels. You make progress at work. You are able to maintain balance between your work, personal, and family lives. You have enough flexibility to respond to surprises or new opportunities.

All time management skills are learnable. More than likely you will see much improvement from simply becoming aware of the essence and causes of common personal time management problems. With these time management lessons, you can see better which time management techniques are most relevant for your situation.

If you already know how you should be managing your time, but you still don't do it, don't give up. What you may be overlooking is the psychological side of your time management skills, psychological obstacles hidden behind your personality.

Depending on your personal situation, such obstacles may be the primary reason why you procrastinate, have trouble saying no, delegating, or making time management decisions.

Ten Commandments for Effective Sales Time Management

Plan your sales time precisely.

Sales time is the time when you're face-to-face with your customers. It's the fundamental reason for your job. Think about it. There is someone in your company who can do everything else that you do. The one thing you do that no one else does is meet with your customers face-to-face. It's the defining moment of your job. It's the part of your job through which you bring value to your company.

Unfortunately, it's very easy to go through the motions of each sales call without taking the time to plan. Most salespeople have only vague sales call plans, if any. I've come to the conclusion that it only takes three minutes to plan a sales call. A daily investment of about 15 to 20 minutes will allow you to thoroughly plan for every sales call.

Make good use of uncontrollable downtime.

You know what uncontrollable downtime is: It's those times that occur without notice, when your day is turned upside down through no fault of your own. It's the time you've driven an hour to keep an appointment with a client you've been wanting to see, who called in sick but nobody told you. The first temptation is to waste that time.

Instead, always carry some work with you wherever you go. That way, you're not frustrated by uncontrollable downtime. In your briefcase, always have some literature about that new product to study, or that quote you need to price, or that paperwork to be completed. By being prepared, you're always ready to make good use of uncontrollable downtime.

Prioritize your activities every day.

In a world that constantly bombards you with things to do, it's incredibly easy and extremely tempting to have your day shaped by the hundreds of demands and requests made by everybody else.

The only real way to take control of all these temptations and interruptions is to create a priority list every day and then stick to that list. That way, you have a clear choice between working your agenda and working everyone else's.

If you have no priority list, then the choice is easy - it's always everyone else's agenda that comes first. At the end of each day, before you go home, take about 10 minutes to create a list of everything you want to do tomorrow. Then go back and prioritize the items in order of importance. Which of all these items is the one that is likely to bring you the greatest result? After that, which is next? Number them in order of importance. Tomorrow, when someone at the office wants you to do something, realize that you have a choice. You can do what they want you to do or you can work on your agenda. Success belongs to the proactive salesperson, not the reactive one.

Constantly evaluate the effectiveness of what you're doing.

As a straight-commission salesperson, I developed a couple of habits that have served me well over the years. One was the habit of asking myself several times during the course of the day, "Am I doing, right now, the thing that is the most effective thing for me to do?"

I can't tell you how many hundreds or thousands of times my answer was, "No." Every time I answered myself in the negative, I had to change what I was doing and do the thing that was the most effective.

My second habit was to always do what's hottest first. What's hottest? Hottest is closest to the money. For example, if I had a choice between seeing one customer and closing the order, and seeing another to do a product demonstration, I'd close the order. That's closer to the money.

Cluster similar activities.

If you have ten phone calls to make, don't make two now, three later, and five this afternoon. Instead, make them all at one time. That way, the amount of time you spend transitioning to the next task will be significantly reduced.

Create systems to handle routine tasks.

We all have routine things that we must do over and over again: fill out expense reports, create sales reports, complete other paperwork, file invoices, review back orders, etc.

You'll find that routine tasks can be handled very effectively if you create a system to handle them and then always use that system to complete the task. You only have to think about the best way to do some of these routine tasks once. For example, if you have to fill out a weekly expense report, always put your receipts in the same portion of your briefcase. Always fill out your form at the same time of the week, in the same place. Again, the duplication of routine efforts makes them mindless tasks. Some things are best done mindlessly.

Use an appropriate strategy for the size and potential of the account.

Some accounts need more attention than others. It doesn't take a rocket scientist to figure that out, but developing that concept into a workable daily routine is something else. Some accounts should get a visit from you every six months and a phone call once a month. Others should get two visits a week. Don't be afraid to use a phone or fax machine to keep in contact with your low-volume accounts. Invest your time in appropriate ways for the potential of each account you have. Do not treat everyone the same.

Don't go into the office!

There is just something about going into the office that is inherently a time-waster. People want to talk to you, you receive phone calls, there's mail to read, coffee to drink and customer service people to chat with. Add that all up, and it's guaranteed to waste your time.

If you must go into the office, and I recognize that sometimes you must, then go in the last part of the day, not the first thing in the morning. If you go in at 4:30 in the afternoon with a half-hour's worth of work to do, you're much more likely to get it done in 30 minutes than if you attempt the same thing at 8 in the morning.

Be conscious of time-wasters, and work to eliminate them.

Time-wasters are unconscious, time-wasting habits you have created over the years. You've become so accustomed to them that you're probably not even aware of them. The first step is to become conscious of them. How many of the common time-wasters on this list are problems for you?

• Taking smoke breaks

• Making personal calls

• Running personal errands

• Not making appointments, just showing up unexpectedly

• Small talk in the office

• Not planning your day

• Reading the morning paper during work hours

Got the idea? You might have a special little time-waster that you've treasured for years. If you're going to be effective in our time-compressed age, now is the time to work to eliminate it.

Don't get caught up in immediate reaction.

Immediate reaction occurs when you have your day or a portion of a day planned, and then you receive a phone call or fax from one of your customers with a problem for you to solve. The natural tendency is to drop everything and work on the problem. After all, isn't that good customer service?

When you do that, you become reactive and lose control of your day. Isn't there some way to provide service but stay in control?

The stumbling block is the assumption that just because someone calls, the problem is urgent and needs immediate attention. So you react immediately. But that isn't always necessary. Often, the situation isn't really urgent and you can address it later.

All you need to do is ask the simple question, "Can I take care of it (fill in the most convenient time for you to do so)?" Often, your customer will say, "Sure, that's OK." On those occasions, you will have regained control of your day and you can proceed with your plan.

Of course, sometimes customers have urgent issues. On those occasions, you do need to take care of the problem as soon as you can. But if you ask the question, a good portion of the time you'll remain in control. By asking the question, you refuse to get caught up in immediate reaction.

Implement these Ten Commandments for good time management, and you'll make great strides in becoming an effective self-manager.

Chapter 2 - Inspiration

> *"Always bear in mind that your own resolution to succeed is more important than any other one thing."*
>
> - Abraham Lincoln

What inspires you? What motivates you? Those are the questions you must ask yourself when you want to go to the next level. I used to travel through neighborhoods and look at dream homes. That would motivate me to get busy. I would read magazines that had the ritzy restaurants that I wanted to go to. I'd watch shows that showed the success I wanted. You must find out what inspires you the most because that's what will give you the reasons to move forward.

A lot of people have a lot to say about selling. They'll tell you their way is the best way to get more customers, the quickest way to get rich, or the only way to success. Deep down, however, we all know the truth – there is no one way to sell. The real secret of selling is to be true to yourself – to sell with honesty and integrity (and a dash of humor) in the way that best fits your unique personality. No one else can do it quite the way you can!

The truth about selling can be divided into two separate but equally important parts – your motive and your method. Your motive is the reason you sell in the first place. What are you thinking when you get up in the morning to go to work? Are you thinking about the paycheck? Are you thinking about your customer's business? Are you thinking about the ways your product or service can benefit the greatest number of people?

There's nothing wrong with thinking about the paycheck – it's a measurement tool that motivates many people. But selling is challenging, and it seems to me that the only thing that makes it easier is a love for what you're doing and what you're selling.

As your success grows, you may confront more people telling you to quit, rather than fewer as you might expect. This is because of one fact – there's less room at the top. It's always easier for people to discourage you than to encourage you. Remember, they're justifying their own lack of success with the same reasoning they're giving you. One of my favorite quotes goes something like this:

"Jealousy is the tribute mediocrity pays to excellence. "

It reminds me of the scene in the inspirational movie "In Pursuit of Happiness," when aspiring stockbroker Chris Gardner (played by Will Smith) tells his son, "Don't ever let anyone tell you what you can't do, not even me." He goes on to teach his son that there are people everywhere who are quick to tell you that you can't reach your goals or achieve your dreams. Because of their own mediocrity and failure these people discourage success. They are jealous of anyone who wants to be or achieve more. And they will do almost anything to bring everyone down to their level.

The problem that faces dreamers is that these people make up the majority of the population. Just think about it. Ninety percent of the people in this world are fighting over the same bone and when a dreamer comes into their midst and says, "You can keep that bone - I'm going to start my own business, I'm going to make president's club, I'm going to get a promotion, I'm going to write a book, I'm going to run a marathon," the horde of mediocre people simply cannot accept it and they immediately attempt to tear the dreamer down with discouraging words and worse, deliberate roadblocks. And when words or roadblocks don't work the dreamer is simply labeled as crazy.

The sad thing for me is that too often these discouraging tactics work to generate self-doubt in people for whom encouragement would have otherwise fueled the fire. Instead of following through on their goals and dreams they give up and go back to their mediocre and unfulfilled life. And then they justify their failure to act by telling themselves that what they wanted was "impossible anyway, they didn't really have what it takes, or that they timing was just wrong." And unfortunately, their wake up one day regretting having never followed through on their true dreams and goals.

So here is my message to you. . . Don't ever let anyone tell you what you can't do. Ever! When you say you can, there will be losers there to say you can't. When you dream there will always be someone there to demand that you wake up. When you believe in yourself there will be others who will try to create self-doubt. When you act there will be short-sighted people who will work to slow you down with roadblocks. And when you achieve, when your dreams have come true, when you cross the finish line with your hands in the air, the mediocre will not welcome you, they will not learn from your example. Instead, the only tribute you will receive from them is their jealousy. But as the mediocre go back to fighting over the same old bone, you will stand on your mountain top, high above the fray, living the life that you deserve.

Chapter 3 – Goals

> *"Obstacles are those frightful things you see when you take your eyes off your goals."*
>
> -- Henry Ford

My mentor taught me to set big goals and some small goals so that you can check them off daily. If you don't have goals you probably have a mediocre bank account. When you set goals, you have a reason to get out of the bed at 5 a.m. Setting goals will ultimately increase your bank account because you will be working more productively toward a more positive result.

The Bible teaches that you should write your goals down and make them plain. I think the reason for this is that it gives you a clear definition of your desire. You see, writing your goals down separates them from all the other things that are not helping you go in the right direction.

Sometimes we wind up in a place we never wanted to go because we start to drift. Goals keep you from drifting. Goals allow you to see the true vision of your destiny. Get yourself a journal and write your goals down in a place where you can see them everyday. Setting goals isn't something to do once a year. Thousands of people write down New Year's resolutions every year and never reach their goals. I've heard people say that they make lists at the beginning of year. There's nothing wrong with that, but what are you doing the other days of the year!

Goals allow you to see what direction you are going. You will need to change them from time to time and add some new ones and check other ones off. Goals will help you fight the procrastination that usually sneaks up on you when you know you should be doing something else. For example, say you have a goal to save for your home and that you will not eat out this month. If you have that written down it will help you make the right choices that will move you closer to your goal. I usually keep a list in my pocket. That way I can pull it out any time and remember what I need to do to make them a reality.

Here's an easy way to remember how to set effective goals. Remember this guideline. Make your goals **SMART**. This means they should be:

Specific
Measurable
Attainable
Rewarding
Timely

Neglect one of these parameters and your chances of achieving your goals drop many times. Why?

The key force that either drives you towards your goals or holds you back is your subconscious mind. Those goal setting guidelines are the necessary criteria for your subconscious mind to accept your goals and start working for you. Otherwise, your mind will work just as hard to keep you in the comfort zone of your present conditions and old habits.

Specific

With a specific goal, you can clearly see what it is you want to achieve, and you have specific standards for that achievement. In making your goals specific it is important that you actually **write them,** which is crucial in all goal setting guidelines.

The more specific your goal is, the more realistic is your success, and the shorter is the path to it. When you work on making your goal specific, you program your subconscious mind to work for you. Then, your feelings and thoughts will lead you to your goal instead of pointing at the obstacles. The more specific your goal is, the more realistic your success is, the shorter the path to it.

Measureable

You need a way to measure your progress and success. This way, you'll know when you can stop and when the goal is achieved. Seeing progress is very important to keep you motivated and enjoy the process of achieving the goal.

Attainable

An attainable goal is a goal for which you see a realistic path to achievement, and reasonable odds that you'll get there. This does not mean that the lower you aim the more likely you reach success. It is well known that goals that work best have a challenge in them. They are chosen as ambitious as possible, but still reachable. Then they will give you more motivation and sense of achievement.

Rewarding

A goal is rewarding when you're clear about why you want to reach it. This is one more place where it is important that the goal is really yours. Have your specific reasons and expected reward in writing. If possible, even with some visual pictures.

Imagine how you are going to feel when the goal is finally reached. This will ensure that the goal is really worth achieving. Then, every time you get stuck and don't feel motivated enough, read your reasons and look at the pictures. This is a known and very powerful practical technique of how to get through difficult moments and not quit.

Timely

The fifth requirement of the SMART goal setting guidelines is that your goal should have a specific time limit. This is also very important for your subconscious mind. Besides, time is the price you pay for the reward from achieving a goal. Setting the deadline will protect you from paying higher price than the goal is worth. This is also your protection from procrastination and perfectionism.

Chapter 4 - Building Your Pipeline

> *"More men fail through lack of purpose than lack of talent."*
> -- Billy Sunday

Your sales prospect list is your pipeline. Your pipeline is also your lifeline in sales. It's always worth your time to build your pipeline. You should always be alert for ways to add numbers to your prospect list. You should always be weeding them out – separating the prospects from the suspects.

Follow-up is also critical. Stay in touch with your prospects and move them step by step toward the sale. As you do this your sales will start to pop out one by one. Measure your success by how many prospects you've added to your list and followed up with daily. You may not get the sale that day but that doesn't mean you have had an unsuccessful day. As you follow up you will close deals that you've had for weeks or even months. The important thing is to push for new business everyday.

If you find yourself just compiling lots of prospects but not getting the sales, it may mean you need learn more about your product. Ask yourself if you are maximizing each prospect by answering their questions and giving them a reason to value your product over the competition. On the flip side, you may be giving out a lot of information but not closing by asking for the sale. Don't waste your time by just handing out information. Be the person who can convey your product with conviction and build value for your product or service.

Your sales pipeline makes you clear about the origin and result of each sale. Every sale starts as a lead; a phone number, a name, an email address, a referral, or someone who walks into your store. After you get a lead, you qualify it, which means you make sure this person is capable of becoming a customer. Do they have the resources for your product? For example, say you're selling mini-vans. A good qualifying question is would be, "Do you have any children?" If the answer is yes, you should try to sell this person. If not, you could try to sell them another vehicle that isn't so family oriented. After you've qualified a lead, you attempt to make a sale. The lead will either become a "continue", an "advance" or a "decline." A "continue" can turn into an "advance" which can turn into a customer -- or a sale.

So a sales pipeline goes like this:

LEAD ---> QUALIFIED LEAD --> CONTINUE/ADVANCE --> CUSTOMER --> REPEAT CUSTOMER

Some products have a short pipeline, while others have a longer pipeline. Generally, the more expensive the product, the longer the pipeline.

An important part of selling is to keep track of the ratios and numbers so you can understand your pipeline and improve it. How many calls does it take to get an appointment? How many appointments does it take to get a sale? And so on. Eventually, you'll find that it generally takes 10 calls to make an appointment and 10 appointments to make a sale, for instance. Then you'll realize that if you made 1000 calls last month and made $5000, then you'll want to make 2000 calls to make $10,000. Once you start knowing your numbers, you start to understand your pipeline.

Suppose you make 100 calls one month and get 20 appointments for the next month, but that next month you're busy going to appointments so you didn't make any calls -- how many appointments will you have on the third month? None. That's because you didn't feed the pipeline.

Of course, if you've done any sales already, you're quick to realize that If you made $20000 in sales this month, it's because you made 2000 calls last month. Or something like that. That's the sales pipeline in reality.

The key to selling is making the calls. You have to get in front of 20 people every day, belly to belly, and talk to them. This keeps your pipeline full. Of course, not all of the calls you make will result in sales, but only calling will make you a success. If you don't want to succeed, don't make a call.

Chapter 5 - Making it up in Numbers

> *Success seems to be connected with action. Successful people keep moving. They make mistakes, but they don't quit.*
>
> - Conrad Hilton

If you're new to this business, you must be willing to make some mistakes - a lot of them. You must be willing to make up in numbers what you lack in skill. Since your presentation and knowledge are not as sharp as a veteran in your market, you have to talk to more prospects to shorten your learning curve. Learn to enjoy this as you learn. Team up with someone who is already getting the results that you desire. Ask them questions about what to say and do.

Don't be afraid to jump right in and go after new prospects. If you want to impress your sales manager and make an income while you're learning your product or service, you've got to get started. Your sales manager may not give you leads if he thinks you aren't a strong closer yet. Create your own leads. Get out and talk to new prospects on a daily basis to reach extraordinary beginning results.

When you're first starting out with a new product or a new boss, chances are you won't be handed a bag of qualified sales leads and told to get to work. You'll have to generate your own leads. Fortunately, there are a number of good sources you can use to come up with leads and make contacts on your own. Here are a few strategies to consider:

The Good Old-Fashioned Phone Book

If you're offering a product or service that is a good potential fit for a business, grab the yellow pages and start making some calls. You may be surprised how easily you can get to the decision-maker within a business. Once you've exhausted the local phone book, fan out to other cities in your area.

It's worth it to take a day and look through all of the yellow page ads for your business category. Make a list of all of the features and benefits your competitors are claiming. More than likely, most of your competitors are only going to list their features. When a feature of a benefit is repeated, put a checkmark next to the one you've already written down, so you don't have to keep writing the same ones over and over.

Next, check out ads in newspapers or other publications where your competitors may be advertising. Make a list of everything that they're saying. Yes, this process will take some time, but it's going to take less than a day and it's critical if you want to generate your first sales and gain a marketing edge.

Once you're finished, examine your list. You'll probably notice that most businesses like yours are saying exactly same thing! So why should a client contact you, as opposed to any other business in your category if everyone is basically saying the same things?

You may say, "Well, I'm better." But how does the client know that? Everyone is saying the same things in the same way. All of the ads look exactly the same. Everyone is copying everyone else. It's what Dan Kennedy calls marketing incest. Marketing incest is when people in the industry keep copying each other until the marketing and advertising gets dumber and dumber and dumber and less effective.

If you look and sound the same as everyone else, you have no competitive advantage. And with no advantages, the prospect is going to make their decision based on price alone. This is what you <u>do not</u> want. You want to stand out. You need to be perceived as being different and unique.

The key word here is *perception.* Maybe you do only offer the standard services, like everyone else. That's fine. But you can frame these features in a way so you're perceived as being different from your competition. So when a prospect sees your ad or calls you on the telephone, you stand out from everyone else. You see, that's what marketing is all about, and that's exactly what this system is about. You're going to discover how simple and easy it really is.

Word of Mouth

This is another great way to generate sales leads. Never be afraid to ask a satisfied customer if he or she knows of someone who would be interested in what you have to offer. Along with the first question, also ask for permission to mention your current customer's name. Often, being able to drop a name will open doors for you that otherwise would remain closed. One of your best resources in expanding your client base will always be a customer who knows and believes in you.

Chapter 6 - Leverage

> *Give me a lever long enough and I will move the world.*
>
> - Archimedes

Leverage will allow you to multiply your efforts by doing something once and creating extraordinary results. If you have a business you can leverage your efforts through employees. In this day and age you can also leverage your efforts through technology. As you become more familiar with your service or product you should look for ways to multiply your efforts. Leveraging should increase your profits many folds because you are multiplying your efforts

It's all about loading up your end of the seesaw. Picture yourself as a kid playing on a seesaw and piling up your friends on your end to lift your opponent high into the air scaring the devil out of him. One way to apply leverage to gain access to your customer is to get people talking about you so that your prospective buyer wants (and feels that he <u>must</u>) talk to you.

Lifting the 2000 Pound Prospect

Most sales professionals aim too low and make the mistake of only contacting one person. This is like sending only one soldier to attack a fortified position. Most salespeople make the mistake of thinking that their contacts within a company only care about the benefits you can offer their company. Don't assume that your contacts are interested in what you say you can do. In reality, they may be much more concerned with their own relationships with the people in power in their company. They're watching out for their own jobs.

Expanding the Circle of Leverage

The solution is called the "Circle of Leverage." Instead of making contact with just one person in an organization, try targeting three or four people in the company who are most important in that person's life.

Imagine a small circle with a larger circle around it. Inside the small circle is the person you want to reach - the person who would most likely make the decision about buying your products and services. The larger circle has four points, at the top, bottom, left and right. The top point represents your target's immediate supervisor, the left and right points are key colleagues of this person, and the bottom point is for this person's top assistant.

Once you have the names and positions of these key people, the next step is to write nearly the same letter to each of the five people you've identified. The letter says "I am writing to you and to (name the other four people) to find the most appropriate person to meet with for a 30-minute appointment. I have these main benefits to offer (name three). When I follow up with your assistant in the next couple of days please let them know if you wish to schedule the 30-minute appointment and what times are good for you. Otherwise, please direct me to the appropriate person you want me to deal with regarding getting together. Thank you. I look forward to meeting you."

The strategy, is to get all the people surrounding your key contact talking about you. If the key contact is asked three times in one day you, he or she is going to feel pressure to talk with you. It's also possible one of the other letter recipients will be impressed with you, even if the key contact isn't. In this case, having five people in the company know about you is better than betting on only one person.

A few days after sending this letter, contact the assistant who works with the person you want to meet. In that call, simply schedule the meeting. The goal is NOT to speak to the key contact directly, because he or she will try to interview you over the phone to avoid meeting with you.

Lengthen Your Lever Through Referrals

Although sales professionals know the importance of using referrals to gain access to their prospective buyers, it's not always used strategically. Some salespeople won't ask for referrals from friends, family, or even clients for fear of jeopardizing their existing relationships. Some just don't know how to do it. I bet if you look at all the marketing tactics you are planning this year, "asking for referrals" is not a line item in your strategy.

I know a salesperson that takes his clients to lunch twice a year. After a nice meal and friendly conversation he asks his client for the names of two or three people who might need his services. He then asks the client to make an introduction through a letter. It just so happens he has a letter written and asks the client to read it and he requests his approval to use it. He also asks if he could pick up some letterhead to print the letter on and get the client's signature.

Focus on events where you can meet people and "leverage" relationships to give and gain introductions to prospective buyers. Ask for handwritten notes of introduction. Every market and industry have organizations, associations, networking, tradeshows, and users groups where you can meet people that can help you gain access to your prospective buyer.

Gather information within the company from the support staff. A great place to get information is from the company's sales organization.

Get acquainted with other people selling to your customers. Sitting in a lobby waiting for a customer one day, two salespeople came in. We struck up a conversation and I learned new information about the prospect I was going to see that helped me position my presentation more effectively.

Don't miss "leveraging" opportunities to load up your end of the seesaw!

Chapter 7 - Outsourcing

> **"No one can cheat you out of ultimate success but yourself."**
> - Ralph Waldo Emerson

Outsourcing job responsibilities can help you free up some of your time for more important tasks. For example, if you need to cut your grass, but you have an appointment that could generate $1000, why waste your time cutting the grass yourself? Pay someone else to do it!

You need to be clear about how much your time is worth. Once you learn to reserve your time for the really valuable activities, you'll be more successful in your work and personal time. You can also outsource work whenever possible. You don't have to do everything yourself. It's not hard to find people who will do a better job than you can on certain projects. These are the ones you should outsource.

For example, I love to write deals, but I don't like doing the paper work. I often hire a personal assistant at about $10 per hour. This way I can leverage my time and focus on more important things that generate a lot more than $10 per hour! This also leaves you less stressed at the end of the day.

Some business owners try to handle everything but get stressed out too early in the game and quit. While its OK to start out by working hard, you should always be looking for ways to do things more effectively through outsourcing. You may not be ready for employees. Hiring full-time employees is time consuming and a big commitment. Instead, look for highly-trained virtual assistants who can do what you need done at a fraction of what it would cost you to hire an employee.

The best candidates for outsourcing are independent contractors with businesses of their own. Such professionals are highly trained and successful in their field and subcontract their talents and services to you on an as-needed basis. This can free you up from large portions of your workload and give you extra time and energy to sell, sell, sell.

Today's technology has made it very easy to outsource all kinds of work via the Internet. Due to corporate downsizing, thousands of qualified professionals are offering their services online as virtual assistants.

You may ask, what's the difference between a regular secretary, personal assistant, office administrator and a Virtual Assistant? The main difference is that a Virtual Assistant is just that, Virtual! A VA completes your projects or tasks at his or her home office, using his or her own equipment, and carries out the work through email, fax, telephone and postal service. Therefore, your VA can be anywhere.

Some services typically offered by VA's are general administrative services, database and web site development, graphic design, sales support, presentation preparation, telephone answering, bill payments, travel arrangements, bookkeeping, desktop publishing, computer training, and medical or legal transcription. Not all VA's offer all of these services. However, by being part of a VA networks, your VA can guarantee client satisfaction by a qualified VA. If your VA cannot complete your task, he or she will find someone who can.

The benefits of outsourcing to a qualified VA are plentiful. VA's only charge for actual time worked. VA's use their own equipment so there is no wear and tear on your office equipment or a need for special equipment. By outsourcing to a VA rather than hiring an in-office assistant, you will never need to pay employment insurance, vacation pay, sick pay, or contribute to retirement plans and worker's compensation.

There is no cost for training new or existing employees; VA's are already qualified. There is no need for extra office space; VA's do everything from their home office. There's no need to worry about in-office employees requesting time off; VA's are available when you need them. Like you, VA's are entrepreneurs and understand the needs of businesses today, ensuring the success of their clients. VA's value each and every client; it is because of these clients that a virtual assistant can ensure the success of their own businesses.

If you already have in-office employees that you cannot go without, a virtual assistant can take a little of the never-ending workload or less-important projects off their shoulders to ensure that your business maintains its quality reputation.

Other functions in your business may require only part-time work. For example if your needs add up to only four days a week in bookkeeping work, then consider outsourcing. This will eliminate the need to hire a full-time bookkeeper. In essence, you pay for the outsourced functions only when you need them.

Outsourcing's advantages will vary with the services, the kind of business you run and, of course, the quality of your provider. It's worth your while to move slowly and commit little by little. Heads-Up: don't sign two-year contracts before testing performance and the relationship.

To get a feel for the process and to accustom your staff to the idea, first try outsourcing one stand-alone project, and then move on to hiring professionals for other areas or ongoing needs.

Chapter 8 - Handling Rejection

> *"Disappointment should always be taken as a stimulant, and never viewed as a discouragement."*
>
> - C. B. Newcomb

Has this ever happened to you? You've just had a great meal at a restaurant and the waiter asks if you want dessert. Your answer is "no." When he hears your answer, the waiter becomes sad and dejected. He looks down at this shoes and slowly walks away. Would you ever expect this to happen? Of course not! Every waiter understands that being rejected in that way is part of their job. Certainly it has no reflection on the waiter's job performance!

This is the attitude you should aspire for in sales. Never get so wrapped up in the decision of a deal that you can't forget it when you leave work. If you know you've done the best you could to contact the lead and give them complete information about your product or service, then you can feel good knowing you've done your best.

The prospect may really want to be sold by you, but they just may not be ready at the moment. If you take the rejection personally now, you could be jeopardizing your chances of selling them in the future, when they are more open. A little persistence at the right time in the future could turn this "No" into a "Yes".

Some of my most valuable clients rejected me several times before they finally purchased my service. Your prospect may have had several salesmen approach them about your product or service. They may have just had a bad experience with another company. This is your opportunity to learn even more about your product so you can target your sales pitch at what makes you different from your competition.

Never argue with a potential prospect. Just listen and count to three if you have to before you respond. Let them know that you understand they may not be ready right now. Ask if there is a better time when you can speak to them. If after several attempts to they are still not willing to listen to you, be pleasant and tell them have a nice day. Remember this is a numbers game, not a likeability contest. Be strong and stand up for yourself, and go get the next one, tiger!

Handling rejection is one of the toughest aspects of sales. Some may find that day after day, knocking on doors and calling prospects blindly is a tough pill to swallow. What makes it even tougher is the inevitable fact that most of the people you come in contact with will be telling you "No!" If you've had the feeling of your heart sinking into your stomach, you are not alone. Over the years, I have been on thousands of sales calls and have certainly lost my fair share. The disturbing part wasn't necessarily the lost sale, but the way I felt afterward. My ego was damaged and I didn't want to speak to anybody. The mere thought of the loss sickened me, and I'm an OPTIMIST! Was there something wrong with me? Why was this happening?

Top sales people understand a simple truth about selling their products and services: Their product will not be a perfect fit for everyone. This point is a critical factor in eliminating your feelings of rejection on a sales call. An important part of handling rejection is the realization that the prospect's decision not to buy is typically not personal, but just business. The best way to look at this is to track your activity and see what your selling statistics really are. Are you closing 1 in 10 appointments or 5 in 10? By knowing this, you can turn those ratios to your positive advantage.

For example, if your ratio is 2 sales out of 10 appointments in a week, that means that 8 prospects decided not to buy. That's okay because you NEEDED the 8 "no's," to earn your 2 sales. Without those 8 "no's" you wouldn't have received the 2 "yes's." The multiple sales that you think you "lost" were actually just stepping stones to take you closer to the WINS you earned. Now, think about a word I just used a second ago, "lost." Isn't it interesting that we feel like we've lost something, when the fact is we never had anything to begin with. How can you lose a sale if you never had it to start?

Another key factor to effectively handling rejection is to change your attitude about the word "NO." This idea may fly in the face of a lot of sales training courses and "how-to" books. The truth simply put is that getting your prospect to a "NO," is a GOOD thing! Read the last sentence again if you don't believe that I said it! There are 4 key qualifications to getting a prospect quickly to a "NO," in the world of sales:

1. They don't have a need or compelling reason to utilize your products or service
2. They aren't committed to fixing the problem
3. They aren't the actual decision maker
4. They aren't willing and able to invest in your solution

If you really think about your last few business deals that ended in a "NO," they probably weren't qualified to work with you in the first place. If a client is going to say "NO" anyway, it's expedient for you to strongly qualify them and to actually push them to a "NO." The word "NO" should actually empower us as sellers to move on emotionally, while saving us time and money by not continuing a pointless cat and mouse game.

Your current attitude and philosophy towards rejection and hearing the word "NO" could be a huge determent in building a successful business. Use the pointers discussed in this article and truly commit yourself to changing your ways for future success and happiness in business.

Chapter 9 - Making A Prospect list

> *"Kodak sells film, but they don't advertise film.*
> *They advertise memories."*
>
> - Theodore Parker

So you have a product that you're excited about. How can you find new prospects and make a sale within the next thirty days? I'll tell you how, you make a prospect list. A prospect list is a list of potential sales. You should start with your warm market because these are people that know you. Warm prospects are friends and vendors that you deal with on a daily basis. This could include your dry cleaner, hair stylist, or dentist. You may not know all these people personally, but where ever you go and whoever you contact could be a potential prospect. Be open to sharing your product or service everywhere.

Since you are already doing business with your warm prospects, their guard is very low and they are looking forward to hearing from you. I create a lot of business from simply telling people I contact in my daily life what I do and trading business cards with them. I've made thousands of dollars in sales in my spare time. I remember once going to get my nails buffed. I simply told the owner the type of product that I was offering and she signed up right on the spot. This happens all the time. Remember, your product isn't printed on your forehead, so its important that you talk about it.

Through all these kinds of contacts, you'll begin to build your prospect list. Your list should be separated in two tiers; 1) friends and family, and 2) people that you do business with on a regular basis. Take out a sheet of paper and see if you can come up with at least 100 names and numbers. Take out your rolodex and click through your phone. Don't prejudge or assume someone is not interested before you tell them what you have to offer. You never know who they know. This is just your grand opening announcement to let everyone know you are in business. Ask your friends and family if they know anyone who would love to purchase your product or service. Get them on board with you. Remind them it would be a shame if their contacts bought the same product from someone else!

Five Myths About Sales Prospecting

For years, I dreaded the prospecting part of sales. The constant rejection was excruciating until I uncovered these fallacies that frustrate many salespeople.

Myth #1: Prospecting is sales.

This is the number one mistake made by small business owners and sales reps. Prospecting is a separate function from sales, just as marketing is distinct from sales but closely linked.

Prospecting is simply discarding all the unqualified leads and retaining the "gold". The job of prospecting is to find qualified leads that may buy your product. Only after this process is complete, should the selling begin.

Myth #2: Prospecting is a numbers game.

The old school of prospecting for business relies on contacting large numbers of cold contacts. However, quality supersedes quantity. You must find prospects that have a propensity and possible motive to buy your product or services.

I know of a large financial powerhouse, who provided sales reps with contact lists for mortgage and investments. The only problem was most prospects lived in a low income area and were highly unlikely to buy any financial product.

Myth #3: Scripts are for kids.

Many sales people insist on prospecting without any script. Scripting provides the framework of a successful prospecting campaign. It allows you to test what key benefits and qualifying questions work. The script must be personalized by the individual so the presentation does not sound "canned".

Myth #4: Prospecting takes time.

Prospecting takes only a few minutes to determine if the lead wants your benefits and can afford your company's product or service. Don't waste time on people unmotivated or unable to buy. Remember to focus on the "gold".

Myth #5: Close them on the appointment.

Far too many sales reps focus on setting the appointment. "Would Friday morning or afternoon, be better for you?" Next week only 20% of appointments show. What went wrong?

Prospects will sometimes find it easier to agree to an appointment rather than saying they are not interested. If a prospect is remotely interested, then offer a much subtler approach...send them an information package. This allows you to build interest and turn the lead from warm to hot.

Sales prospecting done right can have a huge impact on your sales revenue. It doesn't take an armor suit and great courage to deal with the fear of rejection during prospecting. Just keep an open mind to challenge the old school methods of sales and the myths of prospecting.

Chapter 10 - Asking for the Sale

> *"Put it before them briefly so they will read it, clearly so they will appreciate it, picturesquely so they will remember it, and above all, accurately so they will be guided by its light."*
>
> - Joseph Pulitzer

So you've given your million dollar presentation and you're sitting there looking into your prospect's eyes. What's next? Here's what's next: Ask for the sale and shut up! This is decision time and you want them to press that pen to the paper. Your customer wants to be closed. Your confidence in asking lets them know that you are confident in your product. I've met countless numbers of salespeople of all ages who are just order takers. They are simply afraid to ask for the money. You can be good at everything else but this is where it all pays off. You deserve to ask for the sale.

You have to have the attitude that you've just given this prospect information that's more valuable than the price that you're selling it for. If you don't close, you are simply wasting your time and the prospect will go to someone else who can move them to make a financial decision.

There's no perfect time to ask for the sale, but you should most certainly ask after a presentation. The prospect will give you clues that you must pick up on. For example, if a client is asking questions like "How do I get started?" or "What do I need to do?" make an assumptive close and simply start the process of completing the deal.

Children are great at this. As soon as they walk into a store with you, they start planting seeds by asking for what they want over and over again. By the time you make it to the checkout section, you're so exhausted that you at least buy a candy bar for them if you haven't given in already! In your sales presentation, you should do the same - ask for the sale as soon as there is a valid opportunity. Let your prospect know that the time is now.

How many times have you presented your product and service and when it comes down to asking for the money you freeze up? A lot of salesmen shine in their presentation but they lack the skill of properly bringing the prospect to a close. They simply talk to much and the prospect puts them off until someone comes in and properly closes the deal. You must understand that you are not an order-taker. You are here to make a sale, and believe it or not, the prospect wants to be closed. By closing the deal you show that you are confident in your service and feel that you've answered all questions that the prospects have asked you.

I usually say "LETS GET STARTED!" with excitement - then the customer assumes that the right thing to do is to follow your lead. If the customer still has questions, you simply answer them and ask for the sale again. Don't be afraid to ask as many times as you need to, because your show is over and you have others waiting for your next presentation.

Asking for the sale should not be confused with high pressure tactics or being a pushy sales person. If you've done your job effectively, you shouldn't be embarrassed to ask for the sale immediately after your presentation. Sometimes the client will help you close the deal faster if you keep your eyes and ears open. Watch their body language and listen to their words. They might say something like, "What do I do next?" or "What do I need to get started?" That should be your cue to whip out your application and get a signature.

I've seen salesmen young and old who lose opportunities by not effectively asking for the close. Try practicing asking for the sale in the mirror, so that when the time comes you appear bold and confident to your prospect.

We all can use a new sales technique to sharpen up our sales strategy from time to time. Changing your strategy can make the sales more interesting – you won't sound so much like you're repeating a memorized script. I have used and taught this technique. It is very appropriate for retail sales, but it can be altered to work in other types of sales situations. Using this technique will help you determine your customer's buying temperature and will often surprisingly be the catalyst for the close.

Sometimes when we are engaged in a sale, we find that even though we have gone through the sales presentation efficiently, have been thorough in answering all objections and have even narrowed down the make, model or color that your prospect wants, the customer is still not making that buying decision. In other words, we just can't seem to close the sale. It may be that your customer is hesitating for some unknown reason. It could be as simple as that they were planning to go to dinner after talking to you and never intended to purchase right away, or perhaps even that they wanted to use a credit card that they left at home. This is the type of scenario in which you can very effectively use what I call the "Box-Step" sales strategy.

As soon as you have detected that your customer is waffling or stalling on making a buying decision, very politely step away from the customer and towards where ever it is that you keep your product inventory. It could be a stock room, a listing in your manager's office, or an adjacent building -- it doesn't matter, just take a step or two in that direction, then turn back to your customer and say, "Mr. Customer, I'm going to go check my inventory for you (pause)...if I have one in a box (or in stock) should I bring it up for you?" It has been my experience that if you have done everything else right up to this point, your customer will say, "OK -- sure!" If they are agreeable, then you can assume the purchase. Go ahead and bring the item up and write up your sale. It is very rare that you will bring the item up and the customer decides they don't want it. Congratulations -- you made the sale!

However, it may also happen that after you've asked them if you can bring it up, that your customer will tell you "no thanks". If this happens, then do not go to check your inventory, but instead turn and step back towards your customer and continue with where ever you were in the sale. In doing the "Box-Step" sales strategy, now you know how hot or cool your customer is to a decision to buy. Once you have stepped back to them and returned to the sale, you may discover that there was a detail that you missed. If so, resolve the issue and try the "Box-Step" strategy once again and see what happens. Often you will get a "yes" the second time around!

Chapter 11 - A Solid Foundation

> *"Success is the sum of small efforts, repeated*
> *day in and day out"* -Robert Collier

Every good builder knows that a strong structure needs solid support. Without adequate support, any kind of building can be destroyed by wind, water, or other natural forces easily. You've probably seen pictures of tornado or hurricane damage that show the concrete foundation still in place after the rest of the structure is blown away. The house can be built again on the solid foundation.

This is how you must build your business. You must have a solid foundation before you can really start to prosper. You will have wins along the way and you will have losses. Either way, you must continue to nourish the foundational elements of your business. Doing this will create a foundation that can weather all kinds of external conditions.

A key component of foundation-building is to win over your existing customers daily by implementing support systems that keep them satisfied. You should always be looking for ways to strengthen your internal system. Ask yourself how you can provide faster setup and support. The more your product and service satisfies a need, the more competitive you will be in your business niche.

Ninety-five percent of businesses fail simply because they don't manage their systems efficiently. They feel like every dollar should go into the front end of their business system – that is, into new sales. As a business owner, you must have an investor mentality. An investor looks for ways to earn more with minimal investment. Once he has figured this out, he can multiply his profits. Invest only in things that you are really skilled in. Don't invest in something you are not willing to learn about, especially if you don't have a lot of money to invest up front. At least ten-twenty percent of your profits should go into improving your system.

Remember that your goal is to turn your business into a loop. Initial sales, nourished by a tight support structure, will generate more sales through referrals. Sales through referrals are the best kind – they require minimal work from you, and the prospect is already sold on your business because of the recommendation of a trusted friend or business associate.

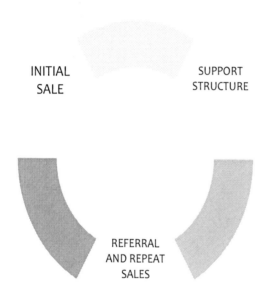

INITIAL
SALE

SUPPORT
STRUCTURE

REFERRAL
AND REPEAT
SALES

This kind of sales leaves you free to concentrate on maximizing your profits. Ask yourself often how you can get your product at a lower cost (e.g. wholesale), how you can expand your product list, and how you can widen your sales audience while still delivering value. Your business system should start from the product to the delivery and on to the continuous contact with your customers that will bring on referrals.

It pays to invest some sweat equity into pounding the pavement and getting some loyal customers on your team. Learn to treat all of your customers as if they were the only ones. This may mean getting up early and getting home late. Your foundation is the key to your dreams.

Whenever you apply for any kind of financing, the merchant pulls your credit report to judge your likelihood of paying on time. Well, your customers don't ask for your credit report. They rate you by your actions. Are you returning their calls? Are you assisting them in a time of emergency? Are you a person of your word? Let them know that you appreciate them by assisting them when they need it. This will give you years of residual rewards for a job well done.

It's critical that you understand the psychology that creates a strong customer base. You know, the kind of customers that are fiercely loyal to you and what you have to offer. Customers like this are indispensable to your success. They drive new prospects to you practically begging that you sell them your product, and they stand as testimonials to your business integrity.

Here are five elements to keep in mind so that the customers you're selling to today become your strong business base in the future:

Finish Strong: It's not the beginning of the customer's interaction with your business that is important. It is the end of the interaction that leaves the biggest impression. The final customer interaction is what resides in the memory of your customer. Ask yourself, what value-added customer service can I provide that will end with a big WOW from customers?

Get the Bad Experiences Out of the Way Early: Customer service based on behavioral science tells us to save the best for last and get the unpleasant side of business out of the way early in the process. This may entail; delivering bad news early or putting unpleasant tasks, such as a lengthy application process at the early stages. Freeing your customers from the bad experiences early, allows them to focus on the positive aspects of your service.

Combine the Pain, Segment the Pleasure: Customer's time perception is linked to the number of breaks in the experience. Smaller chunks of pleasant experiences will be perceived as greater than one large segment. (Disney incorporates this principle by having shorter amusement rides, giving the customer a better experience). Learn to combine your company's unpleasant tasks together and break-up the enjoyable parts of the business process.

Build Commitment Through Choice: Provide your customers with choices in the product or service delivery. A recent study revealed blood donors experienced less perceived pain when they had a choice of which arm the blood would be drawn from. The lesson here is to create choices for your customer during the business process.

Give People Rituals and Stick to Them: Behavioral science tells us that people find comfort in regular, repetitive rituals. Rituals can vary from quick phone call response times to a weekly client progress report. If for some reason, you miss this regular ritual that your customer expects then your customer service takes a big hit.

These five principles of customer service can alter your customer's perceptions forever. Take the time to view the business from your customer's eyes, apply the principles and watch your customer service ratings soar.

Chapter 12 - Pounding the Pavement

> *I learned that the only way you are going to get anywhere in life is to work hard at it. Whether you're a musician, a writer, an athlete or a businessman, there is no getting around it. If you do, you'll win. If you don't, you won't.*
>
> - Bruce Jenner

To make your business a real success, sometimes you'll have to get down and dirty and pound the pavement. You'll have to put your feet to the street. You have to be willing to put some sweat equity into building your empire. Sure, there will come a time when you'll be able to sit in a comfortable office overlooking the city, skyline but you'll never get there without hard work. It's often said, "There's no shortcut to success." Your eventual rest will come as the result of your hard work now, and it will be more satisfying as a result, when you look back at what you've done to get there.

You have to ask yourself how bad do you want this? Are you doing this to get away from that job you hate? Are you doing this to create a legacy for your children? Are you doing this to finally get the car you've always dreamed of? Whatever the reason, you must use it to get you through the early stages. Always keep your goals in view to give you the strength to get through the present. See yourself already driving that Ferrari. See yourself already living in that dream home and this part will become easy.

Learn to enjoy the journey. You'll look back one day and say, "Wow, I remember I had to pound the pavement every day!" You'll be able to take more pride in your masterpiece. You may be rejected, but you must get used to it. Every successful person was rejected at some point in their journey and faced difficult challenges. Your success story will be no different. You will have to face adversity with a passion and desire to reach your goal.

Helen Keller was blind and deaf and reached goals most couldn't even imagine. She knew that although things were very difficult for her, she still had a will and she could make a way. She accepted the challenge and she took it. There's a challenge before you now, and now is your time to TAKE IT!

Starting up a business requires much patience. You can't just open a business with just a snap of you fingers. Don't expect your new business to be an instant hit either. Before you can truly say that it is a success, it must go through several stages first.

The first stage for any start-up business, whether it's direct sales or selling someone else's product is the planning stage. You have to examine the strengths, weaknesses, opportunities and risks that you have in your business. You also have to start introducing the concept of your business to people. In doing so, try to be observant of their reactions and take in all their comments. This will be helpful in tailoring your products and services to your potential customers' needs and wants. This is very important. After all, they are the ones who are going to be buying and using your products and services.

During the first days, don't expect that you will be mobbed with customers. It will take a little while or maybe more time to get your business known to your target customers. Promotions are a great way to get attention. This will entice them to try what you are offering and hopefully, they will like what they are getting. In the long run, what's important is that you are giving them what they need and what they wish for because that's what will make them keep coming back for more.

When you have gained a steady flow of customers for some time, only then will you be able to say that business is a success. It is also important that you maintain the quality of your products and your services. This is a very important component of what your customers like about your brand so you should never compromise it.

Maintaining the success of your business is a much bigger challenge. You should always try to innovate and update every now and then. This will help you keep the excitement of your brand and also help you keep up with your competitors. If you already enjoy what you are doing, it will be easier on you. And whenever you get tired of doing the day's work, just remember how hard you have worked to get to where you are. Don't even consider throwing it all away, because there are others that wish they would have made it as far as you did. I'm sure you would not want to throw it all away just like that. This will keep you motivated and keep you striving hard to maintain your business all the time.

Always remember, building a new business during slow times is never a walk in the park. Here are five reasons why you must make a daily commitment to making it work.

You only know where you're going when you get there.

Things can change so much that you must believe and have faith that they will work out In your favor. You can slowly minimize some risk by incorporating proven techniques that have worked for you or others in the past. Sure it's exciting, but trying to keep people motivated with you can be a big challenge. How Columbus did it I have no idea.

You need to know everything.

You might be able to delegate stuff to experts but really it all falls on you. Especially if your business is about delivering roughly the same stuff as your competitors in a different way, you HAVE to know if the different way is going to work. For someone who doesn't do a lot of detail, this means a lot of learning.

No-one from the normal world gets it.

People on your team who aren't used to this may turn this into self-doubt, as a leader you will have to continually review your plan and see if it's working or you could burn through a lot of cash. Insure them that you are steering the ship in the right direction. When you tell them,

"I'm coming up with a new business model that customers will love," they are bound to give you a quizzical eyebrow raise.

Always challenging can turn into self-doubt.

When you're building something new, you have to continually challenge what you're doing before you burn a lot of cash. People on your team who aren't used to this will turn this into self-doubt - not a good thing.

Some days you're just surviving.

Let's go back to Columbus again. When you get hit with 40 ft. waves in your wooden ship while you're sailing to the other side of the world, you don't really care if you're still heading in the right direction - you just want to be alive! Sometimes you have do stuff for survival that may or may not be taking you down the right path. The thing to do is adjust your plan to deal with the circumstances, but don't get off track. The important thing is to continue to take action.

It's how you get through the tough times that determines whether you'll be successful. Every time I think about those pioneers who set out with literally nothing, and combated nature to go somewhere they had never been, I think, "We've got it easy!"

Chapter 13 - Living Outside Your Comfort Zone

> *"They can because they think they can."*
> - Virgil

Everyone wants to be comfortable, right? Successful entrepreneurs know that success isn't always comfortable, though. You may have to sacrifice some things you like if they are not helping you get where you want to go. People who make comfort a priority never realize their true potential.

It's not always comfortable to pursue success. You have to give up just trying to fit in. You can't just follow the crowd and only read about the people that are making huge leaps toward success. You have to drop your excuses – that you're just not smart enough or tall enough or just not talented enough.

The truth is that many people have become successful with little to no education or special talent. Always go over the reason why you are striving to be number one. Sure, you may not feel comfortable standing in front of a large audience, but if that's what it's going to take, you need to find a way to motivate yourself to just do it. You need to create the courage you need to move forward by visualizing the reasons you're doing this.

It's always uncomfortable to start from the bottom. Always tell yourself the only way is up. There will be times when you'll ask yourself if it's really worth it. Your natural human instinct will say "Maybe I'm just not cut out for this." You must continue to push forward, telling yourself that a little discomfort is a small price to pay for a lifetime of true comfort. The further along you go, the more courage you'll have. Eventually, you'll less of those thoughts, because you will have learned to force them into a small corner.

Sometimes you just have to block out all the distractions around you in order to hang outside your comfort boundaries. This territory is not for the weak. Your friends will call you crazy, and wonder why you're not hanging out at the pub like you used to. You've got to be strong and block out all of the negativity that will come your way.

Ninety percent of all businesses fail within their first five years. How are you going to make sure you don't become one of these statistics? How will you survive your first year, your second, third and fourth? In a global community where competition is fierce, you'll have to continually come up with new ideas in order to stay viable in the marketplace. Learning to stay outside your comfort zone this will allow you to create a new reality that will become your normal reality. You will accomplish more than you ever could imagine!

Starting a small business is one of those huge, life-altering events. Think of it as a marriage; running a successful small business takes the same depth of commitment and desire. As in a marriage, you're going to be living with your business 24 hours a day, 365 days a year. Like any relationship, if you want your small business to be successful, you're going to have to work at it. And it's going to have its ups and downs and surprises.

But on the positive side, if you're the right person with a solid plan, starting your own business can be the most satisfying, exhilarating experience of your life.

The main quality that you have to have to start your own business is a burning desire to do it. Running a small business isn't for the ambivalent or indifferent. How bad do you want to call the shots? How bad do you want to make what you're truly worth?

Look inside yourself and ask these three basic questions before you start your own business:

Do you really want to operate independently and be the person making all the decisions and shouldering all the responsibility?

Are you willing to work hard and make the sacrifices starting a small business entails?

Do you have the self-confidence and self-discipline that will enable you to persevere and build your new enterprise into a success?

If you've answered "no" to any of these, you're probably not ready to start your own business. Overnight success stories are just that... stories. The reality is that success is won through hard work over time. And you want to start and run a successful small business, don't you?

If you answered all three of these basic questions positively, then you're ready to think seriously about starting a small business. But not everyone who wants to start a small business is cut out to actually run a business. Are you enough of an entrepreneur?

If you're going to start a business that has staying power, there are five resources that you must have in place before you open your literal or figurative doors. To turn a start up venture into a successful business, you must:

Fully Commit

Successful entrepreneurs are people who are fully committed to their business ventures. You have to be prepared to put your heart and soul into what you're doing. You have to truly believe in your product or service, and be prepared to work long hours to get others to believe in your product or service, too. You have to be ready to go without treats such as holidays, and even necessities such as salary, for what may seem like an endless stretch of time. And you have to do all this without the safety net that salaried employees are used to, such as benefits and pension plans.

Be a "Type D"

People commit themselves to all kinds of things; causes, hobbies, other people. Just being able to make a commitment doesn't automatically lead to business success. If you're going to get where you want to go in business, and start a business that will endure, you also have to be what I call a "Type D" person; someone who has desire coupled with drive, with strong discipline and determination.

You have to not only have the business ideas, but be able to execute them. Successful business people are tenacious; obstacles are temporary barriers to work around. They may take "No" for an answer, but only for as long as it takes them to reframe the question from another angle and ask again.

But desire and drive alone are not enough to start a business; you don't want your business to be a temporary comet streaking across the sky. Discipline and determination are what give successful business people the endurance to follow through on their business ideas, and weather the storms and calms of the economic climate.

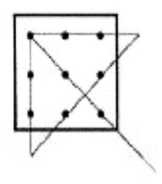

Chapter 14 - Working it Like a Business

> *"Heaven on Earth is a choice you must make, not a place we must find."*
> -- Dr. Wayne Dyer

If you invested $100,000 to start a franchise, you would be there every day, right? You would make sure that you were making progress every day. This is the attitude you must have when starting your new idea or pursuit. You have to work it like a business. You can't put it off and go and do something else whenever you feel like it.

You need discipline and a spirit of sacrifice. You won't feel like doing certain things, but to get the results you want, you have to do the ground work even when you don't feel like it. Remember, your idea is valuable and you have to work it as that. Put aside some time to concentrate on your business. If its part time, do it. If its full time, do it. Don't delay working your idea.

The sacrifices you make today will pay off in huge dividends in the future. You will get out of your business what you put into it. You'll be planting seeds that will began blooming at different stages. Be honest with yourself. Are you really putting your all into the time you've saved for your business? I see people all the time who sabotage their success by doing less than they could be doing. For example, have you ever seen someone at the gym sitting next to the weight machine talking on their cell phone? Don't tell me, let me guess – the person was overweight, right? How much do you want to bet they spend more time on their cell phone at the gym than working out?

This time it's focus time - no distractions allowed. The same effort that you put into building someone else's dream now has to go toward building your own. If you're working from home, prepare a designated area that you can work effectively from. This means a space where you can focus on your work with no distractions. Only when you've focused diligently will you see the results that you desire.

Your key is in your plan. Every successful business has a plan You can avoid the consequences of poor or no planning if you are aware of these common pitfalls:

Putting it off.

Don't wait to write a plan until you absolutely have to. Too many businesses make business plans only when they have no choice in the matter. Unless the bank or the investors want a plan, there is no plan.

Don't wait to write your plan until you think you'll have enough time. "There's not enough time for a plan," business people say. "I can't plan. I'm too busy getting things done." The busier you are, the more you need to plan. If you are always putting out fires, you should build firebreaks or a sprinkler system. You can lose the whole forest for paying too much attention to the individual burning trees.

Cash flow casualness.

Cash flow is more important than sales, profits, or anything else in the business plan, but most people think in terms of profits instead of cash. When you and your friends imagine a new business, you think of what it would cost to make the product, what you could sell it for, and what the profits per unit might be. We are trained to think of business as sales minus costs and expenses, which equal profits. Unfortunately, we don't spend the profits in a business. We spend cash. So understanding cash flow is critical. If you have only one table in your business plan, make it the cash flow table.

Idea inflation.

Plans don't sell new business ideas to investors. People do. The plan, though necessary, is only a way to present information. Investors invest in people, not ideas.

Don't overestimate the importance of the idea, particularly the importance of the uniqueness of the idea. You don't need a great idea to start a business; you need time, money, perseverance, common sense, and so forth. Very few successful businesses are based entirely on new ideas. A new idea is much harder to sell than an existing one, because people don't understand a new idea and they are often unsure if it will work.

Fear and dread.

Doing a business plan isn't as hard as you might think. You don't have to write a doctoral thesis or a novel. There are good books to help, many advisors among the Small Business Development Centers (SBDCs), business schools, and there is software available to help you (such as Business Plan Pro, and others).

Spongy, vague goals.

Leave out the vague and the meaningless babble of business phrases (such as "being the best") because they are simply hype. Remember that the objective of a plan is its results, and for results, you need tracking and follow up. You need specific dates, management responsibilities, budgets, and milestones. Then you can follow up. No matter how well thought out or brilliantly presented, it means nothing unless it produces results.

One size fits all.

Tailor your business plan to its real business purpose. Business plans can be different things: they are often just sales documents to sell an idea for a new business. They can be detailed action plans, financial plans, marketing plans, and even personnel plans. They can be used to start a business, or just run a business better.

Diluted priorities.

Remember, strategy is focus. A priority list with 3-4 items is focus. A priority list with 20 items is something else, certainly not strategic, and rarely if ever effective. The more items on the list, the less the importance of each.

Chapter 15 - No Shortcuts to Success

> *"The entrepreneur builds an enterprise; the technician builds a job."*
>
> *- Michael Gerber*

There are no shortcuts on the road to success. You know the old saying, right? "No pain, no gain." This has to be one of your mottos on the way to success. If your mind is made up, however, you've won half the battle. You've chosen the path to success. You will reap rewards.

We've all seen infomercials late at night that tell you there's an easy way to the top. The problem is, these ads only give you the canned version of what you really have to do to achieve success. Some business lessons have to be learned the hard way. The up side is that when this is the case, the pursuit becomes more challenging and the success is more enjoyable.

Even if you have to experience lots of uncomfortable situations up front, think of it as a test to see if you really deserve what you're going after. When I faced challenging situations in the past, I would imagine that the gods were watching me to see how I would deal with them. "Does he deserve it?"

The testing proves how fast you will give up. Give up and you'll never see the reward. If you continue to push forward, you'll receive the reward because you've paid the price to receive it.

Consider the children of Israel in the Old Testament. They were destined to be blessed, even though they moaned and complained about everything. They complained about the food, the weather, and the leadership. Many of them perished without seeing the good land that God had promised them because they didn't appreciate what God had done for them.

The lesson here is that you've got to appreciate where you are NOW. Learn to appreciate that customer that call you and asks you the same questions over and over. Appreciate that customer that you had to call ten times before you got the deal. Appreciate the opportunity that youv'e been given, and work it daily. You have to enjoy the journey as you climb to the next level. You don't know – the reward could be right around the corner, but if you stop now you will forfeit your destiny. It could be that top floor office overlooking the city skyline. You could be the CEO of the fastest growing company in America.

Continue to press forward and never look back. All of the events that have brought you to this moment have not been a mistake. Your whole life has already been planned. Everything that you've done up to this point has prepared you for this occasion. It will all come together as you continue to take the road less traveled.

Chapter 16 - Rolling up your Sleeves

> *Failures do what is tension relieving,*
>
> *while winners do what is goal achieving.*
>
> - Dennis Waitley

So it's time to roll up your sleeves and make some sales! If you don't have any new sales leads, the reason may be that you're still going after the same prospects you talked to last week. You've got to learn how to separate the "start now's" from the "start later's." This way, you'll shorten your path to the close. You must seek new prospects on a daily basis.

I used to list my clients' names and all their contact information on 3x5 index cards. If the prospect wasn't ready one day, I'd just note it on the card and call the next scheduled day. Sometimes I'd call the prospect ahead of time just to see if they were serious about keeping their appointment. I'd carry my prospects in my pocket. I'd separate the cards into two stacks – "warm" and "hot." The hot stack would be prospects who showed immediate interest in my service and were qualified leads. The warm list would be clients that I'd already seen and were either still thinking about doing business or still shopping. I'd check on them daily as well.

I'd still work to add new prospects every day. You can't get too comfortable with only the prospects that you have at a given time. You should continually be adding fresh names and numbers to your database. I also learned that if I had too many prospects in my pocket and no sales, I just wasn't closing like I should be. I was just collecting prospects but not following up or asking for the sale like I should. So with this in view, I'd go back and contact my prospects with the latest information, and do my best to bring them to a close. So roll up your sleeves and add more prospects to your list while staying organized and following up so that you're maximizing your sales opportunities.

Strategize for success

In today's economy, big and small businesses are seeking every opportunity to win sales through competitive advantages. Smart owners of small businesses know a sales strategy can create a competitive advantage.

No matter what the size of your business is, selling consists of two main functions - tactics and strategy. Sales strategy is the planning of sales activities, including methods of reaching clients, competitive differences and available resources. Tactics include day-to-day selling - prospecting, sales process, and follow-up.

The tactics of selling are very important but equally vital is the strategy of sales. The advantages are too compelling to ignore.

Competitive Advantages of Strategic Sales Planning

Increased closing ratio by knowing clients hot buttons
Improved client loyalty by understanding needs
Shorten the sales cycle with outside recommendations
Outsell competitors by offering the best solution

Triple-tiered Sales Strategy

The development of any type of plan begins with research. The insight gained for a competitive advantage comes from the marketplace not from your mind. The approach to use is what I call "Triple-tiered Sales Strategy". Look at your client and the outside influences on their business. Approach all three tiers to understand your customer.

Tier 1: Associations: What associations does your target customer belong to? Contact the membership director and establish a relationship not for selling but to understand their member's needs.

Tier 2: Suppliers: Identify non-competitive suppliers who sell to your customer. Learn their challenges and look for partnering solutions.

Tier 3: Customer: Work directly with your customer and ask them what their needs are and if your business may offer a possible solution.

The 7 Habits of Business Success

Habit 1. Cultivate Inner Networks: Entrepreneurs practicing the art of business success know the power of networks. They take the time to identify and build relationships with key peers, mentors, and advisors. This inner network provides support, direction, and an increased number of people to assist. Having an inner network of five people who have a network of five more, grows the network exponentially.

Habit 2. Customer Centric: Business success requires an unwavering commitment to the customer. This commitment encompasses a mindset of understanding the customers' world. Understanding the customers wants and needs provides the business with a greater opportunity to earn a loyal customer base. Focus away from business and profits, and toward what you can do to improve the life of your customers.

Habit 3. Humble Honesty: Business success requires the ability to know your strengths and weaknesses. Being open and honest about yourself and your business creates growth as an individual and as a company. Don't spend time developing weaknesses. Find help for weak areas, enabling you to focus on strengths. In the book, "Now, Discover Your Strengths", Gallup Organization reveals that building our strengths instead of fixing our weaknesses is the path to mastery and success. Take the time to know yourself and business.

Habit 4. Adaptability: Business success requires the ability to adapt to changing situations. Nothing ever goes as planned. The world of business is full of surprises and unforeseen events. Using the habit of adaptability allows business owners to respond to circumstances with the ability to change course and act without complete information. Being flexible allows us to respond to changes without being paralyzed with fear and uncertainty.

Habit 5. Opportunity Focused: Problems are a regular part of business life. Staff issues, customer misunderstandings, cash crunches- the list is endless. To achieve business success, look at both sides of the coin. Every problem has an opportunity. Being opportunity focused makes the game of business fun and energizing.

Habit 6. Finding A Better Way: Productivity is the cornerstone of business success. Formulate the habit of finding a better way to make your business more productive. This will create more time to focus on the critical issues that drive sales and profit. Productivity can be enhanced by technology, automation, outsourcing, and improving business processes.

Habit 7. Balanced Lifestyle Management: A business can consume an owner's time and energy. It's easy to allow the business to take control of your life. Business success requires the habit of balancing all aspects of your life. Separating time for daily business tasks, profit driven tasks, and free time is a habit that will make your business and life more enjoyable. Take the time to plan each week.

Learning and instilling new habits in your daily business life can have a dramatic effect on your level of success. Review each of the 7 habits. Choose one habit to focus on for a month or until you achieve mastery. Gradually incorporate each of the 7 habits of business success into your life and attain your business dreams.

Chapter 17 - Ideas Create Money

> *"Success does not consist in never making blunders, but in never making the same one a second time."*
> — Josh Billings

Don't ever minimize the worth of your ideas. To be successful in today's fast-changing marketplace, you need to continually create ideas for your next marketing plan. Keep educating yourself and reading powerful business literature that will expand your thinking. Subscribe to publications that cater to your industry type. Have the attitude of a student; continually learning new skills and techniques to grow your business. You should also attend business seminars or webinars that keep you motivated and keep your imagination expanding.

I keep motivational tapes and CDs on hand in my car and listen to them when I'm driving. This makes the time I spend in traffic valuable, profitable time. When I listen to business mentors who have been successful, my brain cells are energized. Before I know it, I'm on fire and moving in the right direction.

I also keep a journal handy to write down new ideas. My mentor advised me to never trust my memory, because you can easily forget that fresh new idea. If you write it down you can always refer back you it when the time is right. Don't be afraid to turn those ideas into reality. Just take action in growing your business it doesn't always just take money. If you have the right idea you can draw people to you that are willing to invest in you and your dream. If you have a sales team, it's your job to come up with different contests and incentives to keep them motivated. Some salesmen don't necessarily get motivated by money. You can help them reach their goal by creating an objective that pushes them to work harder. Your income – as well as theirs - will grow substantially as you create new challenges for them to reach.

Think success. To attain the kind of success that you want, you need to dream big. Every success story starts with big dreams. You need to have big dreams for yourself - which you want to be somebody rich, famous or fulfilled. You need to have a clear vision of what you want to achieve. But it doesn't stop in dreaming alone. You should actively visualize success in your mind that you can almost feel it, touch it or it is within your reach. Play this image back at every opportunity. What does it feel to triple your current income? How will your life change? What will your business look like if you achieved the million-dollar mark?

Successful entrepreneurs possess an attitude of openness and faith that you can have what you want if you can simply envision it as the first step on the path of action to acquiring it. Management gurus have taught us the power of visualization - seeing yourself in your mind as having accomplished your dreams. If you want to be a successful writer, envision yourself signing books for a throng of people who have lined up to have your autograph. If you want to be rich, picture yourself in luxurious surroundings holding a fat bank account. And the process of envisioning success for you should be a constant activity! You need to think that you are successful (or will be one) every single waking hour. A personal development coach shared me her secret to help her continuously visualize her goals for the moment: when climbing stairs, recite your goal with every step you take. So if you want more money, say "I will have money" in every step of the stairs. This technique will reinforce your goal and keep it fresh in your consciousness.

Be passionate with what you do. You start a business to change any or all parts of your life. To attain this change, you need to develop or uncover an intense, personal passion to change the way things are to live life to the fullest. Success comes easily if you love what you do. Why? Because we are more relentless in our pursuit of goals about things that we love. If you hate your job right now, do you think you will ever be successful at it? Not in a million years! You may plod along, even become competent at the tasks, but you will never be a great success at it. You will achieve peak performance and do what you have to do to succeed only if you are doing something that interests you or something that you care about. Entrepreneurs who succeed do not mind the fact that they are putting in 15 or 18 hours a day to their business because they absolutely love what they do. Success in business is all about patience and hard work, which can only be attained if you are passionate and crazy with your tasks and activities.

Focus on your strengths. Let's face it; you cannot be everything to everybody. Each of us has our own strengths and weaknesses. To be effective, you need to identify your strengths and concentrate on it. You will become more successful if you are able to channel your efforts to areas that you do best. In business, for example, if you know you have good marketing instincts, then harness this strength and make full use of it. Seek help or assistance in areas that you may be poor at, such as accounting or bookkeeping. To transform your weakness to strength, consider taking hands-on learning or formal training.

Never consider the possibility of failure. Ayn Rand, in her novel The Fountainhead, wrote, "It is not in the nature of man - nor of any living entity, to start out by giving up." As an entrepreneur, you need to fully believe in your goals, and that you can do it. Think that what you are doing will contribute to the betterment of your environment and your personal self. You should have a strong faith in your idea, your capabilities and yourself. You must believe beyond a shadow of a doubt that you have the ability to recognize and fulfill them. The more you can develop faith in your ability to achieve your goals, the more rapidly you can attain it. However, your confidence should be balanced with calculated risks that you need to take to achieve greater rewards. Successful entrepreneurs are those who analyze and minimize risk in the pursuit of profit. As they always say, "no guts, no glory."

Plan accordingly. You have a vision, and you have enough faith in yourself to believe that you can achieve your vision. But do you know how to get to your vision? To achieve your vision, you need to have concrete goals that will provide the stepping-stone towards your ultimate vision. Put your goals in writing; not doing so just makes them intangible fantasies. You need to plan each day in such a way that your every action contributes to the attainment of your vision. Do you foresee yourself as the next Martha Stewart of hand-made home furnishings? Perhaps today, you need to see an artist to help you conceptualize the new line of hand-made linens that you hope to launch. Intense goal orientation is the characteristic of every successful entrepreneur. They have a vision, and they know how to get there. Your ability to set goals and make plans for your accomplishment is the skill required to succeed. Plan, plan and plan - because without planning, failure is guaranteed.

Work hard! Every successful entrepreneur works hard, hard and hard. No one achieves success just by sitting and staring at the wall every single day. Brian Tracy puts it out this way, "You work eight hours per day for survival; everything over eight hours per day is for success." Ask any successful businessperson and they will tell you immediately that they had to work more than 60 hours per week at the start of their businesses. Be prepared to say goodbye to after-office drinks every day – and regular weekend get-away trips. If you are in the start-up phase, you will have to breathe, eat and drink your business until it can stand on its own. Working hard will be easy if you have a vision, clear goals, and are passionate about what you do.

Constantly Look for Ways to Network. In business, you are judged by the company you keep - from your management team, board of directors, and strategic partners. Businesses always need assistance, more so small businesses. Maybe the lady you met in a trade association meeting can help you secure funding, or the gentleman at a conference can provide you with management advise. It is important to form alliances with people who can help you, and whom you can help in return. To succeed in business, you need to possess good networking skills and always be alert to opportunities to expand your contacts.

Willingness to Learn. You do not need to be a MBA degree holder or PhD graduate to succeed in your own business. In fact, there are a lot of entrepreneurs who did not even finish secondary education. Studies show that most self-made millionaires have average intelligence. Nonetheless, these people reached their full potentials achieved their financial and personal goals in business because they are willing to learn. To succeed, you must be willing to ask questions, remain curious, interested and open to new knowledge. This willingness to learn becomes more crucial given the rapid changes in technologies and ways of doing business.

Persevere and have faith. No one said that the road to success is easy. Despite your good intentions and hard work, sometimes you will fail. Some successful entrepreneurs suffered setbacks and resounding defeats, even bankruptcy, yet managed to quickly stand up to make it big in their fields. Your courage to persist in the face of adversity and ability to bounce back after a temporary disappointment will assure your success. You must learn to pick yourself up and start all over again. Your persistence is the measure of the belief in yourself. Remember, if you persevere, nothing can stop you.

Discipline yourself. Thomas Huxley once said, "Do what you should do, when you should do it, whether you like it or not." Self-discipline is the key to success. The strength of will to force yourself to pay the price of success - doing what others don't like to do, going the extra mile, fighting and winning the lonely battle with yourself.

Chapter 18 – Vision

> *"Being rich has more to do with a picture than a bank account... it is all about the picture you see in your mind about your life... that determines what's in your bank account."*
>
> - Doug Firebaugh

Sales managers who have vision can predict the future – simply because they create it! Vision is innovating a *purposeful, organized* search for change. It is not for the timid. Vision has elements of invention, entrepreneurship, curiosity, and adventure. The sales manager whose focus is on next Friday's paycheck is obviously not a visionary.

There is, no doubt, an element of risk in being a visionary. Not every corporation welcomes a visionary, and not every visionary fits into a corporate mold. However, those who are fortunate enough to be a member of a visionary company know that there is no limit to achievement. Sales managers with vision have no horizons, and the corporation that shares such a vision does not stand in the way to the pot of gold at the end of the rainbow.

What are the secrets of sales managers with vision? They are long-term oriented – they think long-range. They can look five to ten years into the future as clearly as the narrow-minded can see to the ends of their noses. On the pragmatic side, visionary sales managers are able to assure themselves with an incentive-based contract that pegs remuneration to imagination.

Everything starts with a vision: finding a good hire, motivating a team, or creating a successful sales presentation. The difference between average communicators and inspiring leaders is the latter frame their vision around a grand purpose. Express goals that enlarge people's vision. The massive coffee chain, Starbucks, began as a small Seattle store selling coffee beans. It took the CEO's vision to create "a third place" between work and home where customers could sip lattes, espressos, and cappuccinos.

Imagine you're on a crowded company bus. It is a dark rainy night so you can't see outside. The bus is on a winding mountain pass. You notice the bus driver is not sure where they are going and both the headlights and wipers aren't working. As scary as this may sound, it is exactly how some sales people feel with directions from sales management.

If a company has a united vision for growth, everyone works better together. Unfortunately, many companies and organizations choose not to share a vision for growth. When this occurs, the sales team has no direction and must determine where and how they will find customers. If they don't know where they are going, any direction will do. Naturally, this makes reaching sales goals impossible. Having a clear vision for success is critical for sales management.

Turn the High Beams On

Sales people are more likely to deliver the right type of customer when they know what management is looking for. Better yet, if the organization offers sales incentives and a clear profile for new accounts, the sales team becomes motivated. Sharing a clear vision is like having clear windows and turning the high beams on. Everyone knows what to look for and how to get where they are going.

Creating A Vision Is Easy - It Only Takes Two Steps.

The first step is to imagine you are sitting behind the wheel this time. Because it is still dark, you turn on the high beams to light up the highway as far as you can see. You think about the entire journey. You list your goals and map out the entire route. You use a voice recorder to describe the sales route with clear details. Most importantly, you must take pictures along the way and draw your vision of the journey and destination.

The second step is a little different. You must sit in the back of the bus this time and take the journey as a quiet and restrained passenger. This time the drivers will only use your notes and drawings. Fortunately, you have an opportunity to share your vision of the journey and destination with the driver.

When you are finished with this exercise, you will have a clear vision of sales growth mapped out for your sales team. Giving them a copy of what you drew and tell them what to look for provides the direction they need. One of the advantages of doing this exercise is that now, if anyone joins your company, you can share the vision of where you are going and provide a map of how to get there. Good Selling.

Chapter 19 – Upselling

Don't ever lose a chance to tell your clients about the other products that you offer. You should always be trying to up sell something new after your initial sale. The customer likes you and trust you and is willing to make another transaction with you. Up selling will increase your bottom line and increase your customer loyalty. If the customer knows that they can get everything that they need from someone they can trust, you will make more money.

People often regard *up selling* and *cross-selling* as sales techniques: sales strategies to increase sales. Yet each has a customer service component to them as well. I prefer to think of them as forms of both sales *and* customer service.

When a customer calls to purchase one product or service, and you offer them a better, more appropriate or more versatile product, you are fulfilling *additional* needs. That's a form of service!

When you receive a call from a current or potential customer, your full array of products and services is often at your customer's disposal. By employing your listening skills, asking pertinent questions, and thus better understanding how they intend to use your product(s), you may uncover additional needs, more elegant solutions or advantageous strategies they may employ. You're delivering service when you cross sell or up sell.

Let's review a typical interaction. A customer calls with a stated need.

You, as a **knowledgeable rep,** know the product lines best: their strengths and weaknesses. You've done your homework and know all of your products' and services' capabilities and compatibilities.

You, as a **skilled listener and problem solver**, understand their needs and can make informed recommendations. You ask closed-ended questions to determine a baseline of pertinent information; you ask open-ended questions to elicit details of the customers' experience, intentions and understandings.

You, as a **persuasive and skilled rep**, can make the additional sale. Listening to their current needs and anticipating future needs, you can identify products or services to solve tomorrow's dilemmas as well as today's problems. You may even show customers better and more innovative ways they can conduct their business.

In the course of these conversations you may offer them training or consulting to accompany their sales, companion products to accompany their primary purchase, or other additional or more powerful tools and services for success.

Suppose that you are selling transaction commerce systems by telephone from a call center. As calls come in, follow these techniques:

Ask Questions to Uncover Needs:

"What is your greatest current need in a system?"
"What is your current volume of business?"
"How much do you project your business will grow in 12-18 months?"
"How big is your department?"
Listen Intently:
Listen to what they say. Take notes.
Listen between the lines to what they're implying. What picture does it paint?
Confirm your comprehension of their situation by paraphrasing for agreement.
What are their critical issues? Price, compatibility, ease in upgrading, etc.

Know Your Product Line:

Be familiar with the strengths and weaknesses of each product.
Understand which accessories work well with each primary product.
Be clear on your profit margins when proposing different/additional products.
Know "Migration Paths" for graduating to newer or better models.
Recommend "add-on" products to enhance utility of their existing products .
What's new? Put another way, what don't they know about yet?

Propose Solutions:

Recommend sets of products that past customers have raved about.
Cite past successes in recommending suites of products, add-ons for customers.
Speak the language of Benefits instead of just stating Features.
Emphasize value instead of price. Reliability, reputation, warranties, etc.
Anticipate concerns and allay their fears with positive statements about each.

Action Steps:

Post your product list and match accessories to products with magic markers.
Role play the conversations and uncover new needs.
Work backwards! Pick a product and figure out ways of leading customer conversations toward this product as a solution! (Step one: what are the benefits of this product? Step two: what "itches" can this benefit scratch? etc.).

Chapter 20 - Attitude

> *"It is your attitude, not your aptitude, that determines your altitude."*
> - Zig Ziglar

Are you excited, pumped up, enthused and ready to Rock and Roll? This should be your attitude when you wake up in the morning. Sometimes it will be a challenge, but you must genuinely affirm these things in response to any negative emotions or feelings that you may have. It's your attitude that will make this a great day.

Always start your day by reading something inspirational, or listening to an uplifting message while in the shower. Think of the challenges that you'll face today. You've got to be ready to fight them off in order to make the best decisions. Many things will be vying for your attention - radio ads, friends, billboards, e-mails. That's why it's important to get your attitude ready to handle any situation that may arise today. Attitude is a big part of getting the results that you desire.

Stellar sellers and successful entrepreneurs usually have certain distinct personality traits. Many success stories can be traced back to basic enthusiasm, which makes an impression on prospects who've become used to the same-old, same-old hackneyed pitches. A great closer will possess an aura of competence and zeal that puts him at the top of the board each month.

Experts and business owners agree about the basic personality characteristics that allow a salesperson to transcend mediocrity.

Creativity - Having an appreciation for the non-obvious solution is a must if a sales pro is going to outpace the pack. While an average salesperson depends on business cards and leave-behinds, a true rainmaker brings a unique vision to his work that makes him stand out.

Passion - Genuine love for a product gets salespeople through the inevitable dark times, and it makes their offers all the more irresistible to their clients. Passion, like creativity, cannot be faked, so it has great weight with customers.

Integrity – Why is it that used-car salesmen are so mistrusted? Because the perception is that they lack integrity and that they'll say anything to get the sale. The old saying is, "Customers buy the salesperson." When your customers sense that you're a person with integrity, they feel good about their purchase. Trust makes your customers today repeat customers in the future. People today are more nervous than ever about salespeople's' integrity. You need to do whatever you can to let your customers know that you are honest.

Tenacity - Shelving feelings of rejection to keep plugging away is another essential requirement for sales success. It takes personal courage to get up every morning and say, "I am going to be the best." It also requires a certain steely quality to persist in the wake of one dismissal after the next. Sales requires someone who can always see possibilities, even in difficult situations.

Commitment - The sales cycle for any big deal can typically take months, even years. Keeping an eye on the prize, while continuing to sell to other prospects simultaneously, takes commitment. You must have a burning desire. To a large degree, sales success is the result of the salesman's willingness and intent to make things happen.

Chapter 21 – Prime Time

> **"It's never too late to be what you might have been."**
> \- George Eliot

It's prime business hours, and your competition is sitting around drinking coffee and reading the newspaper. But not you. You have your eyes wide open looking for the next deal.

Many, many salespeople waste the most valuable hours of their day being unproductive. You must learn to focus on closing prospects during your prime time. All your other tasks should be done during after primetime hours. For example, if you know you should be doing 20 – 30 presentations to new prospects every day, then keep your focus on that. Don't use your prime business hours to drop off your dry cleaning, go grocery shopping, or watch your favorite soap opera. This is when you should be selling for top dollar. This is the time when you should be presenting your product or service to new prospects or taking care of valuable customers.

Time management will help you put everything in proper perspective. You should be doing paper work in the evening or at a non primetime period when you don't feel rushed and can concentrate on just that.

So how do you identify prime time? It's easy. Primetime starts when your prospects are opening their doors and ends when they are closing. If you want to see even greater results, push a little harder even after hours. Some of your prospects may be available for appointments in the evenings or on weekends. The trick is to be ready at all times, with your pen in your hand, just waiting to write a deal. Be prepared with your sales material - you never know what time might be deal time.

These time management secrets will help you stay in control:

Get Aggressive About Managing Time

Time and money are both critically important in business. Yet most business people give more specific thought as to how to spend their money. Too often, how we spend our time is only thought of in terms of "What am I going to do today?" or "What should I do next?"

Just as a well-run business should carefully develop a strategy to determine how to spend its money, an effective businessperson should carefully develop a strategy to determine how to use his or her time.

Just as a well-run business follows a budget in spending money, an effective businessperson should also follow a budget (or schedule) in spending time.

Prioritize Your Time

The first step in effective time management is not to develop a schedule, but instead to develop a time strategy. The time strategy should be based on a short list of time priorities.

Start by identifying the number one way you can most likely increase profits by use of your time; then the number two way; then the number three way. This short list of time priorities should form the foundation for your time planning for every week of the year.

These time priorities may be identical to key parts of your company strategy or they may be different. For example, if your company strategy is based upon excellent customer service, spending lots of your time in customer service may not be the best use of your time if you have a terrific customer-service manager.

Narrow Your Focus

Focus is crucial for time management, and the fewer priorities you focus on at once, the more productive you will be.

After you have your major time priorities for the year established, you should allocate them by week or by month. Like it or not, a lot of our time each week is going to be eaten up by non-strategic items that we have no control over; hence it is important to limit the number of strategic time goals we have for each week. So even if you have ten strategic time goals for the year, you may want to focus on no more than one or two of them in any given week.

For example, in a particular week you may plan on working on your number one time objective, let's say planning improvements for the company's major product line, and a secondary goal, let's say re-evaluating the dealer marketing program, but no time on other secondary time goals that you plan on tackling during other weeks.

Set Aside Uninterrupted Time

Every week you should make up a detailed time plan, which you modify each day as needed. Except in times of crisis, try to make sure day-to-day issues don't push your strategic time priorities off your schedule.

Generally your major strategic time priorities will involve such activities as planning, thinking, and developing ideas. More so than day-to-day issues, such activities require big blocks of uninterrupted time.

Constant interruption kills any hope of effective time management. One way to avoid interruption is to make it clear that when your door is closed you are not to be disturbed. Another is to have regular meetings, such as every week, with the people that you interact with the most and insist on saving non-pressing issues for these meetings.

Time Traps

Stay on guard against these potential time wasters:

Spending a disproportionately high amount of time in the offices where the most congenial people are, as opposed to where the most important issues are.

Wasting too much time getting daily updates on routine activities as opposed to waiting for a more meaningful weekly summary.

Jumping too eagerly into the routine, more straightforward work and putting off the more complex and difficult work.

Not starting the more important work first thing in the morning.

Not bothering to make up a schedule for each day.

Over scheduling--scheduling each day so tightly that it is impossible to stay on track and the schedule quickly becomes meaningless.

Chapter 22 - Its Showtime!

> *"A real entrepreneur is somebody who has*
> *no safety net underneath them."*
> - Henry Kravis

Your nails are polished, your smile is bright, and you're dressed for success. Its show time! It's time to shine and show the world what you're made of. This is important no matter if you're in outside or inside sales. Your customer wants to know what can you do for them today. How can you bring value to their business? You must play your part to the tee to get the award and earn a lifelong fan.

The crowd is watching to see how you respond to the objections. You respond with confidence because you know your product inside and out and when you don't have an answer, you say, "No problem, I'll find out for you." Then you'll watch the confused look on your customer's face turn into a smile. You'll ask for the sale and the customer will give a ready "Yes."

Whenever you give a presentation, you must see it as a show with you as the starring actor. Everyone wants to be in the movies – now is your chance to be in the spotlight. But this is not a stage. This is the real world – your Emmy and your Oscar are the residual rewards of customers and referrals.

When an actor goes in for an audition, they are judged based on their ability to persuade a crowd. There are many "salesmen" out there, and your customer has seen them come and go. They are waiting for the one who will give an award-winning presentation and make then want more.

It's not always price that wins a new customer. Listen carefully to your customer. Listen for the clues in the words that they speak. Watch for clues in their body language. If your customer's hands are folded, fold yours. If they cross their legs, cross yours as well. Do what you need to do to find out what your customers have been missing and let them know that you are the new blockbuster hit that they don't want to miss.

Can you close a sale in just seven seconds? You can do it faster if you use a sales technique to make a great first impression. Seven seconds is the average length of time you have to make a first impression. If your first impression is not good you won' t get another chance with that potential client. Make a great first impression and the client is likely to take your small business seriously.

Whether your initial meeting is face-to-face, over the phone or via the Internet, you do not have time to waste. It pays for you to understand the sales technique of how people make their first judgment and what you can do to control the results.

Learn the Non-verbal Sales Technique: When you meet someone face-to-face, 93% of how you are judged is based on non-verbal data - your appearance and your body language. Only 7% is influenced by the words that you speak. A good sales technique is to remember people do judge a book by its cover. When your initial encounter is over the phone, 70% of how you are perceived is based on your tone of voice and 30% on your words. It's not what you say - it's the way that you say it.
Choose Your First 12 Words: Although research shows words make up a mere 7% of what people think of you in a one-on-one encounter, don't leave them to chance. Express some form of thank you when you meet the client. Perhaps, it is "Thank you for taking your time to see me today" or "Thank you for joining me for lunch." Clients appreciate you when you appreciate them.

Use Their Name Immediately: Another forgotten sales technique is to remember there is no sweeter sound than that of our own name. When you use the client 's name in conversation within your first twelve words and the first seven seconds, you are sending a message that you value that person and are focused on him. Nothing gets other people's attention as effectively as calling them by name.

Pay Attention to Your Hair: Your clients will. In fact, they will notice your hair and face first. Putting off that much-needed haircut or color job might cost you the deal. Don't let a bad hair day cost you the connection.

Shiny Shoes Sales Technique: People will look from your face to your feet. If your shoes aren't well maintained, the client will question whether you pay attention to other details. Shoes should be polished as your sales technique. They may be the last thing you put on before you walk out the door, but they are often the first thing your client notices.

Walk Fast: A faster walker can be perceived as important and energetic - just the kind of person your clients want to do business with. Pick up the pace and walk with purpose if you want to impress.

Chapter 23 - Your Best Year Ever

> *"Nothing can stop the man with the right mental attitude from achieving his goal; nothing on earth can help the man with the wrong mental attitude."*
>
> - Thomas Jefferson

You can make this year different than last year. This time next year you could be driving a new car – living the lifestyle of your dreams. The only thing that's holding you back is yourself. Stop imagining that things will just happen on their own and make them happen today. Today can be the beginning of your best year ever!

Your best year ever starts as soon as you put procrastination and excuses aside. Things and people are not holding you back, you are. When you finally realize this fact, you'll begin to see progress immediately. You will wonder why you haven't done this sooner. The results that you'll see will motivate you to go on. You'll learn how to repeat your winning strategy. Don't feel like you have to wait for the next New Year's Eve celebration or your birthday to make resolutions for change. Your future depends on the choices you make today. For things to change dramatically you must change dramatically. You can start by doing little things at a time. Make a list of goals that you want now and another one for things that you want for the next month.

If possible, create a chart that allows you to reflect on your goals every day. Your life will start to change – you'll feel the rewards immediately as you work toward more long-term goals. If you like things the way they are now, then don't bother to change. Nothing will change! Sales reps come to me all the time and say, "How do you think my week's going to be?" My answer is usually the same: Unless you change, nothing else will change. You've got to increase your numbers, even if you are just learning about your product.

My life started to change the day I decided enough was enough. I made a clear choice to do things differently than I did before. After that, my account began to grow by leaps and bounds. When you start to do things differently, you may face opposition. Understand that this is only a part of your new growth. Your destiny is only reachable by choice, if you choose not to reach for it, you'll never reach your full potential in life.

A truly successful life involves doing the things that bring the most enjoyment to your soul. Knowing that you had a part in creating the success will make you more confident in handling challenging times when they arise. Once you get through a challenging time, you'll be empowered to do it again. Everyone on earth has challenging times when they must be strong. Once you realize that challenges only come to make you successful, you begin to look at problems differently. Now you understand that you need problems in order to be successful. What is success without problems? We would have to call it something other that success!

By becoming a skilled problem-solver, you'll learn how to achieve results each time. Some people live to get through the day, but wouldn't it be better if you tried to live to get something out of the day? Success is getting something done today that you've been putting off. When you overcome your procrastination, whatever it is, you'll feel the thrill of success.

It's the small choices that are made every day over time that add up little by little to success. Remember how you learned to ride a bike when you were a kid? One step at a time, right? One fall after another. Eventually you were pedaling away. Make up your mind to make this a successful day today no matter what day it is. You no longer have to postpone your happiness to Friday or Saturday. Your success begins today and in increments you will have a successful year.

Chapter 24 - Banking on Your Goals

> *There are only two words that will always lead you to success. Those words are yes and no. Undoubtedly, you've mastered saying yes. So start practicing saying no. Your goals depend on it!*
>
> *- Jack Canfield*

Don't fall back on excuses like "I can't succeed now, the market is bad." What about your personal market? Are you spending your money wisely and making the best decisions for your family and your wealth building? Even in a so-called "bad market," things are still being sold, someone is still getting rich in your area. Ask yourself what you can do to be that person. Are you going to slow down because your favorite presidential candidate doesn't win? You have to make up your mind that you will succeed no matter who's in office or how many bad decisions Congress makes. Your ultimate success depends on your personal market. Are you strengthening your skills, or just making excuses like "Nobody's selling."

What about you? You can be the **one** that's selling while everyone else is running for cover. When I made over thirty thousand dollars in one month I had gone through many emotional roller coasters. There were times when I wanted to give up and walk away, but when you give up, you forfeit your reward and someone else gets it. Don't forfeit your career or your future. Continue to be active in educating yourself so that when it's down time for everyone else it's profit time for you!

When you go after your goals, you push up your income up as well as your progress. I had come a long way from making five dollars an hour to making over $30,000 in one month! My success came gradually as I made and went after my goals. Even if you lose it all after you've gotten there, your winning life-strategy can work for you for ages. Eventually you'll earn it back.

Chapter 25 – Faith

> *"Faith is a knowledge within the heart, beyond the reach of proof."*
>
> - Kahlil Gibran

The Bible says that if you have the faith just the size of a mustard seed, that you can move a mountain. To the natural mind, that's impossible. I think that when the Creator Himself said those words, He wanted us to use our natural powers to create success before it even happens. If you can imagine success before it even happens, you are halfway there.

Everyone is challenged with difficult decisions – some more challenging than others. Faith allows us to imagine our way through it all. The Bible also says we should strive to be perfect. It's interesting to note that it doesn't say we will reach that point. It just says to strive. If you have faith that you will make something happen and you strive to go after it, it will become reality.

We've all heard the stories of people who became successful by striving to be the best in their field. All of them dreamed they would succeed, and eventually they reached their goals. The same thing applies to everyone's goals in life. You must have the faith that your dreams will come true. Position yourself to strive toward them daily.

I remember when I had just moved to a new city and was practically penniless. I had been working on a commission salary, so I wasn't guaranteed to make any income unless I had made some sales. I hadn't closed any sales in about two weeks, and I needed to make one soon or I'd have to look for a new job. But I loved what I was doing at the time so I persisted.

I kept on meeting prospects every day, and followed up with them as usual. I told myself, "I've got to get a sale soon or I won't be able to put gas in my car to make it to my next appointment." Somehow, I was just crazy enough to keep on going. Just at the point when I felt like giving in, finally I got a sale.

That experience never left me. It was this that taught me the importance of sticking to it, even when things get rough. It would have been easy for me to give up and go back to something easier – something less challenging. Faith is proved when it's put to the test. Faith empowers you to push your boundaries – to scale new heights. As you progress toward success, your faith will grow. It will get you through your next challenge, and the next and the next. Keep your faith and believe that you will succeed!

Chapter 26 - Fighting Procrastination

> *"There are a million ways to lose a work day, but not even a single way to get one back."*
>
> ~Tom DeMarco and Timothy Lister

How many times have you told yourself that you will just do it later when you know you should do it today? I used to wonder why the Bible teaches us not to procrastinate. The answer I've arrived at is this: If we put something off until tomorrow, we miss the blessing that's available to us today. If you could just stop your procrastination every day for the next year, you'd be reaching your goals daily.

Our days would be so much more fulfilling if we didn't procrastinate. Procrastination only pushes you back. Think about what it would be like for a child to get pushed back to the same grade every school year. He is supposed to be going on, but he keeps failing year after year. Eventually he accepts failure as a way of life.

Procrastination can cost you in your wallet and even in your physical and emotional health. Procrastination usually lowers your self- esteem as well. When you see someone with something you like or wish you had, you'll feel negative because you feel that somewhere along the line you could have had the same reward if you just hadn't procrastinated. Procrastination causes us to pass up opportunities that could change our future.

The good news is that procrastination can cease anytime you're ready. You can face procrastination today by saying you're going to get it done today no matter what. When you're faced with a choice about how to spend your time, make the productive choice that will have a positive effect on your future. Of course you can't get there in one day, but gradually you'll see change, and you'll see yourself moving to the next grade.

Once you've graduated from procrastination, your attitude will change automatically. You'll be so excited about the accomplishments you've made that you'll never want to stop. Your income will grow as well. Now nothing can stop you. Remember, just one sales call could make a difference. Your next presentation could be the sale you've been waiting for. The next e-mail you respond to could change your life.

You deserve the best life possible and procrastination only prevents you from gaining it. But you must also learn to be patient. You won't attain all your goals overnight. But if you don't start today, for sure you will never have a chance to reach them at all. What a tragedy it would be to know you could have lived your dreams if you had only not procrastinated!

Procrastination. Putting off what you can do today until tomorrow. Seven years, five months, and two days later you're wondering why you never started that book. It would have been done by now and you would be reaping the rewards. Writing would be your full-time pleasure now. You can see yourself sitting on the garden patio of your dream home surrounded by towering palm trees and luxurious flowers. You look across the Pacific as the ocean air gently blows across your face. The phone rings. Your latest book made the Best Seller List.

Funny how in regret the picture is always bright and sunny, and in procrastination its doom and gloom. You think, "No one will ever want to read my book. No one will ever publish my book." What if you could switch that picture so you are pulled to the vision like it was a magnet. The vision will be there. Why not make it sooner rather than later. Procrastination results in stress, poor health, and regrets that can last a lifetime. Taking action leads to fulfillment, life experience, and wisdom. So read on to discover how to break through procrastination, take action, and make things happen.

Step 1- Where in your life are you procrastinating? Is it the appropriate decision to delay or irrational postponement? Choose one project that you want to stop procrastinating on.

Step 2- Discover the source in order to create a solution. Consider when your car doesn't start. You look for the source of the problem. When you find the source it is easy to take action to make the repair. Look behind procrastination to find what is stopping you. It may be an unpleasant task, lack of interest, someone else's goal, a large overwhelming project, fear, poor time management, or indecision. When you discover the source you are one step closer to making a change. Congratulations!

Step 3- Based on the source decide if this is a goal you want to keep. If so, choose a strategy that makes you more comfortable. Below are some examples to get your creativity flowing. However, choose what is right for you. You will have to develop new habits. Best to create habits you want vs. what someone else wants for you. Discover the source and set the strategy up in a way that you know you will take action.

An Unpleasant Task/ Lack of Interest- Schedule it at the beginning of the day so it is not hanging over your head all day long. Think of how great you will feel to have it done. Reward yourself when you follow through.

Someone Else's Goal- Set a boundary...say no or accept only the part of the job that you feel good about. If you can not say no (ex. employment situation) then you may choose to follow the above solution.

A Large Overwhelming Project- Break it down into small manageable tasks. What part can you do? What part can you delegate? What is the first small step you know you can do right now?

Chapter 27 - Organizing Prospects

> *"First comes thought, then organization of that thought, into ideas and plans, then transformation of those plans into reality. The beginning, as you will observe is in your imagination."*
>
> - Napoleon Hill

Organizing your prospects will save you a lot of time. By Identifying and categorizing your prospects according to where they are in the sales cycle, you'll be able to narrow your focus to your more productive prospects. It's a really good idea to invest in management software that allows you to track the progress of your prospects.

My method of choice is index cards, which I carry with me all the time and keep updating. I separate them into these categories: "General follow-up," "Hot follow-up," and "Really hot follow-up." You should be constantly cycling your prospects. As prospects turn into customers, you should stamp the card and store it in your "Prospects sold" box. You should also make plans to contact that prospect after they have received their product or service and thank them for doing business with you.

Many salespeople feel like once they get the signature on the dotted line that the sale is over. Really, this is only the beginning. Sure, you've been rewarded for closing the sale, but now you must nurture that prospect by tracking your contact with the customer for the life of the agreement. This includes calling them on birthdays, sending out newsletters, or sending thank you cards to let the customer know how much you appreciate their business.

Think of yourself as your clients' bodyguard. You must protect your investment. You have time and energy invested in these customers that could never be replaced if you were to lose them. Why not fight to keep your customer satisfied with your service? You will be rewarded many times over if you show your customer that you are dependable and trustworthy after the initial sale has been made. You will begin to develop a fan club of customers who are loyal to only you regardless of what the competition tries to offer them. You will be the person they call for advice and guidance even in personal matters. It's only when your foundation is solidly built with loyal customers that you will really start to build wealth in your opportunity to service them.

Even if you are new to follow-up, it is the most important aspect of your job. To get the edge, you have to think about what you can offer that your competition can't. How can you make your product stand out in the crowd? What makes you different? Many salespeople sell themselves short by using the excuse that the market is saturated. If you're bringing value and distinction to your product line, you have something to offer that the others can't. You can capitalize on your edge by staying organized and offering better service.

Organize Now!

It's time to get organized, but you just don't know how or where to begin. You are stressed out and feeling out of control. And you keep putting it off (we call that procrastination), hoping it will just go away.

It's time to get real. While you are sitting around thinking about getting organized, opportunities are rapidly passing you by. Businesses are expanding, the competition is moving ahead effortlessly, and you are still struggling with internal situations that are preventing you and your business from moving forward. Now is the time to make the necessary changes within your organization so that you will be prepared to move into the future.

There are eight basic principles you should use now to get organized. Let these principles work for you to boost and maintain your productivity.

Determine your goals. You must know where you want to go so that you can have a plan for how to get there.

Use a calendar system. It can be electronic or paper, but it should have delineated time sequences. This way you can schedule your time each day and be able to see exactly how you are spending your time. Many people like to use a 'block' style calendar. That is one with a block for each day to be filled in. This is really a poor method for managing your time. You will be much more productive using a calendar with definite time increments. This way you can schedule your time more accurately.

Create activity stations for all of your office equipment. You should have the following stations in your office: telephone, computer, supplies, current files, reference, stationery.

Categorize your files from general to specific. Learn how to maintain a filing system that will support your work style. General topics may include: medical, financial, insurance, automobile, warranties. Specific categories may include: medical/Mary; insurance/life; insurance/car; warranties/large appliances.

Use a spiral bound notebook near your telephone. Record all messages in the book. This will eliminate all the scraps of paper and sticky notes that seem to line our desks. As a bonus, it creates a permanent log to refer back to.

Process mail daily. Learn to use the 'FAT' system and incorporate into your life: File, Act and Toss. Make a decision about each piece of paper as you read it.

Develop a paper management system that you understand and commit to using. Paper usage has increased greatly and will continue to be in our offices daily. The sooner a system is put into place, the more control you will regain.

Finally, maintenance is the key. Once you have organization back in your life, 5-10 minutes of daily maintenance will provide you with a stress-free lifetime of achievements.

Don't be too much of a perfectionist – you might make your system too complicated. Don't procrastinate – you'll just put off creating the system. Don't overdo it – you'll take on too many tasks. Most entrepreneurs are dreamers which is good. But dreamers also have to take their eyes off the big picture and actually do the nitty gritty tasks that will create the ultimate goal.

Learn to take one step at a time. Try a new habit every few weeks. It takes 21 days to learn a new habit; give yourself the gift of time. Give yourself permission to learn new habits and to experiment until you find what works for you.

Chapter 28 – Networking

> **"There is only one success--to be able to spend your life in your own way."**
>
> - Christopher Morley

Networking is a popular business concept that can take many forms. It can include attending events to pass out literature. You can network through chat rooms and e-mail. Networking allows you to make a potential prospect into a warm lead. Networking allows you to maximize meetings, conferences and even social gatherings by contacting people you met within 24 hours of the event. This shows your prospects that you're serious about business.

When you make such a contact, call or e-mail the prospect saying that it was a pleasure meeting them, and if they have a need for your service to contact you. Attach your contact information and any other relevant marketing material. Most people just attend events but never truly get the benefits of networking because they never truly follow up. Even if the people you contact aren't interested, you can always ask for referrals. These people have met you personally and have a sense of you as a person. People know people who know people. The referral process is the best way to build up your customer base. You may even want to offer an incentive, discount, or other promotion in exchange for referring business to you.

Don't forget that the people you're contacting may well have businesses of their own. You may be able to work out a business relationship that brings profit to both of you. Ask questions: Learn their needs and find out what is working for them.

Some Tried and True Techniques -

There comes a time in every small businessperson's life when common networking practices like handing out business cards, attending various meetings and talking up potential clients only goes so far. Eventually, the same old techniques get overused to the point that they become insufficient.

But how many times have you gained new business, created a great relationship or watched your website hits skyrocket because you did something unusual? Or uncommon? Perhaps even unexpected? Maybe you were on the right track.

The following is a list of atypical networking techniques that will help boost business. WARNING: They will stretch your courage, they will test your expertise, and they will challenge your creativity. But when business cards aren't enough, alternative ways to develop and maintain mutually valuable relationships are your ticket to networking success.

What's Your Story?

How did you get your start in business? Did you "fall" into your line of work? Perhaps there was an interesting anecdote, epiphany or event that caused the birth of your business. If so, this is called "Your Story." Now, it's not your Elevator Speech or your 30 Second Commercial. It's your story. And it's a fundamental tool for helping people and potential customers get to know you.

Here's the key: Write it out. Practice saying it aloud. Make it funny. And tell it to everybody. Not only does this create a memorable presence, but the more you share it with people, the more they will share Your Story with other people. Why? Because people don't remember things, they remember stories. And after a while, the word about Your Story will spread.

Mix the Medium and Wow People

When I receive an email from an organization or business who has a question, wants to work together or just wants to chat, I do something called "Mix the Medium." Here's how it works:

1) The exact moment I finish reading the email, I obtain the person's phone number (if I don't already have it.) If there's no email signature, I look at their email address or go to their website. If all I know is their company, I call Directory Assistance or look them up on City Search. Basically, I do anything I can to get their phone number within the next two minutes.

2) Then I call them right back.

3) I then say, "Hi - I was in the office when your email came through and I thought I'd call you back!" I say with a big smile on my face.

PEOPLE LOVE THIS. I have never done this without completely blowing the caller away. They respond with such excited phrases as "Wow, that was fast!" or "I'm impressed you called back already!" In fact, I recently received an email from a friend of mine who just changed jobs. He was writing to say hello and wish me a Happy New Year. And since I hadn't heard from Jake in quite a while, I Mixed the Medium and called him right back. Five minutes later he booked me to do one of my speaking programs for his new organization!

Network en Masse

Speaking of speaking, here's another untapped networking resource: local groups, organizations and associations. But I'm not talking about joining; I'm talking about giving a speech. It's what I call "Networking en Masse."

Small businesspeople are successful because they're experts on something. So whether you're in sales, printing, tech consulting or retail, find a way to transform your expertise into an informative, concise and entertaining speech that will help other people like yourself boost business.

Contact the meeting coordinator of local clubs and organizations. They always need speakers. Offer the group a free 15-20 minute program. Include valuable tips, stories, illustrations and examples from your own business experiences that are of interest to the members. By speaking, you position yourself as an expert, validate your credibility and increase your company's visibility.

Chapter 29 - Creating the Right Ad

> *"If you wish success in life, make perseverance your bosom friend, experience your wise counselor, caution your elder brother, and hope your guardian genius."*
>
> - Joseph Addison

It's worth some time and energy to make sure you come up with the best business ad. Take a whole day to research the ads your competition is running. Search through local phone books and newspapers and phone directories from nearby towns as well. On a pad of paper, make a list of all of the features and benefits your competitors are claiming. More than likely, most of your competitors are only going to list their features. When a feature of a benefit is repeated, put a checkmark next to the one you've already written down, so you don't have to keep writing the same one over and over.

Yes, this is a laborious process. But it's going to take less than a day and it's critical if you want to have a marketing edge.

Once you've done this, examine your list. You will notice that most service businesses like yours are saying exactly the same thing! So why should a client contact you, as opposed to any other business in your category if everyone is basically saying the same things?

"Well," you may say, "I'm better." But how does the client know that? Everyone is saying the same things in the same way. All of the ads look exactly the same. Everyone is copying everyone else. It's what's called marketing incest – when people in the industry keep copying each other until the marketing and advertising gets dumber and dumber and less effective.

If you look and sound the same as everyone else, you have no competitive advantage. And with no advantages, the prospect is going to make his or her decision either by calling only one person or, even worse, on price. You need to stand out. You need to be perceived as being different and unique.

Again, the key word is *perception*. Maybe you do only offer the standard services, like everyone else. That's fine. But you can frame these features in a way so you're perceived as being different from your competition. So when a prospect sees your ad or calls you on the telephone, you stand out from everyone else. You see, that's what marketing is all about, and that's exactly what this system is about. You're going to discover how simple and easy it really is.

Sometimes we are clearer about how to do something when we know what NOT to do.

Here are some sure-fire ways to waste your advertising budget!

Ignore Your Target Audience
If you don't want any customers, be sure to ignore your target audience. Don't worry that you're trying to sell scooters for the elderly in a teen magazine. Your target audience doesn't really matter, does it?

Knowing your target audience is crucial to any successful ad campaign. Always identify your potential customers before beginning any work on your ad campaign.

Don't Let the Pros Handle Your Materials
Save a buck and create your own materials. It won't make that much difference right?

There's a reason people hire ad agencies, freelance copywriters, freelance graphic designers and production houses to handle their ads. You're an expert in your field and they're experts in their fields.

Writing that brochure on your own and printing it out in black and white on your printer may sound like a good idea to save money. All it will do, though, is make your company look unprofessional.

Copywriters are specifically trained to write content that sells. Graphic designers are trained to create eye-catching materials that make your company stand out. Taking a stab at it yourself may sound like a good idea but the selling message will suffer and your company will lose sales.

Plans? Who Needs Plans?

Just start advertising willy nilly without really thinking about your budget and the right places for you to advertise and you're sure to blow your ad campaign quickly. Every successful ad campaign begins with a well-conceived plan. From identifying the target audience to knowing exactly where you need to advertise, your plan is a must for your ad budget to be spent wisely and your potential customers to be turned into paying customers.

Run That Ad Just Once

Your ad is so great, you only need it to appear once to make a huge splash. Whether it's a commercial or a print ad, just run it once and you'll instantly blow your ad campaign. Frequency is the key. When you know your target audience, you also know where you need to advertise. How often you run the ad makes a big difference in if the ad will be effective. One ad won't do the trick. It's better to run that one print ad multiple times than just once if you really want to gain customers.

Who Needs Consistency?

Trash all of your hard work on an ad campaign by making each ad different. Who needs the same tag line in every ad? Who wants the logo to look the same every time?

If you're not keeping your materials consistent, you're not making an impression with customers. The more people see your logo, your tag line, even the same colors in your ads, the more they'll begin to associate your company and products with the place they need to be spending their money.

Chapter 30 - Pricing your Products

> *"A failure is a man who has blundered, but is not able to cash in on the experience."*
>
> - Elbert Hubbard

Pricing your products is a critical and tricky factor in any kind of sales. You have to know what your profit points are. This means you have to know how low you can go with a prospect before agreeing to provide a service or product. Remember that you are working to make a profit, so it's very important that you maximize your efforts and time by using strategies that increases your profit margins. You should always know what your competition is charging.

You may not be directly affected by your competition's low prices if you offer an exceptional service in addition to your product. Frequently my competition offers the same product that I do for a lower cost, but since I provide better communication and customer care than the competition, I'm able to charge more for my service. Basically, I can ask for more because I provide more value to my customers than the competition.

You should always be trying to locate your competitions' weak spots. Then you can maximize your efforts in the same area and provide what they are not. If you can provide a service that can enhance a person's lifestyle and offer exceptional service along with it, you will live your dreams and have an endless supply of new customers. Your customer base will grow exponentially through referrals.

A successful entrepreneur never shortchanges the small things like keeping his word, returning calls promptly, and responding to even the smallest needs of the customer. In exchange, he receives huge rewards. It's your customer who will put that new Mercedes in your garage of your dream home!

Your goal is to make price less of an incentive to your customer and keep them focused on the value that you will provide for them. If you can focus them correctly, it won't matter if your competition offers their product for free – the customer will go with you because all they want is to know is that you will be there for them when they need you the most.

Never make a sale in fear, and never let your prospect or your competitor make you sell your product in fear. When you sell in fear, you lose confidence and concentration. You lose your control and domination of the situation. You could end up making a decision that you won't be able to stand behind, and ultimately you may lose the sale altogether.

If a customer tries to test you by telling you the competitor's price, don't be afraid to walk away. But before you do, look them straight in the eye and make sure that they are comparing apples with apples. Sales managers are under pressure to get sales in and often they have to make low ball offers to attract customers. Most of the time they strip features from the product in order to sell at that price. This may include stripping away valuable services and benefits that the product would otherwise offer.

Everyone has seen the ads that show a fully-loaded new vehicle at a low price. Sure, you want to rush out and buy it, but what they aren't telling you is that you would actually have to pay for all those extras. It's the same with your service. If you realize that the price your customer is aiming for is way too close to your profit margin, ask yourself if further bargaining is even worth your time.

Don't ever feel bad about making a profit. Some salespeople feel guilty if they make a profit; maybe they're just not cut out for sales. Without profit, you can't run your business, so learn to play up your superior service and persuade your customer positively, so that he feels good when he pays for it. Sure, others may charge less, but if your service is unique, it's worth a premium. Always look for ways to increase your value and raise your prices when necessary. Implement systems that increase the effectiveness of the offer.

Pricing Strategies for Success

The pricing strategy of your small business can ultimately determine your fate. As a small business owner you can ensure profitability and longevity by paying close attention to your pricing strategy.

Commonly, for many small businesses, the pricing strategy has been to be the lowest price provider in the market. This approach comes from taking a superficial view of competitors and assuming one can win business by having the lowest price.

Avoiding the Lowest Pricing Strategy

Having the lowest price isn't a strong position for small business. Larger competitors with deep pockets and the ability to have lower operating costs will destroy any small business trying to compete on price alone. Avoiding the low pricing strategy starts with looking at the demand in the market by examining three factors:

Competitive Analysis: Don't just look at your competitor's pricing. Look at the whole package they offer. Are they serving price-conscious consumers or the affluent group? What are the value-added services if any?

Ceiling Price: The ceiling price is the highest price the market will bear. Survey experts and customers to determine pricing limits. The highest price in the market may not be the ceiling price.

Price Elasticity: If the demand for your product or service is less elastic, you can then have a higher ceiling on prices. Low elastic demand depends on limited competitors, buyer's perception of quality, and consumers not habituated to looking for the lowest price in your industry.

Once you understand the demand structure in your industry, review the costs and profit goals you have in your business plan. The low price strategy is best avoided by small business, but there are conditions such as a price war that can drag a company into the lowest price battle.

Evading a Price War

A price war can wreak havoc in any industry and leave many businesses, out of business. In the early 90's, such a price war took place in the fitness equipment market in one large American city. Profits were plentiful but a price war took the gross margins from 42% to 12%. In less than 18 months, over 60% of the retailers were out of business. Use these tips to evade a deadly price war:

Enhance Exclusivity: Products or services that are exclusive to your business provide protection from falling prices.

Drop High Maintenance Goods: There may be products or services in your business that have high customer service and maintenance costs. Drop the unprofitable lines and find out what customers don't want.

Value-added: Find value your business can add to stand out in the marketplace. Be the most unique business in the category.

Branding: Develop your brand name in the market. Brand name businesses can always stand strong in a price war.

Leave the price-cutting and price wars to big business. Small businesses with solid pricing strategy can escape a price war and low price position. Carefully consider your price decisions. Your business depends on it.

Chapter 31 - Negotiating

> *"I cannot give you the formula for success, but I can give you the formula for failure--which is: Try to please everybody."*
>
> - Herbert Bayard Swope

When you're looking to sell something, it's important to possess strong negotiation skills. Not everyone is good at negotiating—many are intimidated. For those who do not like to negotiate, but want to perfect their sales skills, here are some ways to help you overcome your fears and become a successful negotiator:

Understand your product/service value. Before you try to sell anything, it is critical that you know and understand your product line and its inherent value to your customers and prospects. Interview current and previous customers to determine the marketplace viewpoint of your product/service.

Your previous customers will give you quite a bit of ammunition for fending off your competitors' products and services, as they will be able to tell you your weak points and your competitors' strong points (in their eyes). You have to be open-minded and willing to accept the criticism, and use that criticism to develop stronger value for your product/service line in order to gain the advantage in selling to potential customers.

Know your competition. Research and study your competition. Know what they are selling and how it is working for them. Understand their price points and their perceived advantages to your prospect base. Also—know that some of your current customers are likely shopping around. Keeping your competition in your hip pocket will help you continue to develop products and services that provide value to your customers, and will keep you strong at the negotiating table.

Know your sales strategy. How will you sell your products and services effectively? Know your strategy before you begin negotiating. You don't know how well your purchasers will have done their homework in advance, so have backup plans for your backup plans. Make sure you put your strategy to paper and put it into action with each opportunity to negotiate a sale. The better and stronger your strategy for selling your products/services, the better positioned you will be to come out ahead when negotiating with a prospect.

Understand your buyer and their motivation. Know your niche market so well that you understand a buyer's motivation before they come to you. Each buyer will be different in what motivates them to buy—but based on past experience in selling your product or service, you will have a general idea of their motivation. Ask key questions to further draw that out, and make sure you pay close attention to how they answer your questions. Their answers will always determine your next steps in the negotiation process.

Don't talk price—talk value. The buyer may bring up price right away. You need to talk value. Make sure you point out the value of your services/products without mentioning price, especially if you are a price leader. It is very important that the customer understand the value of your products/services if you intend to negotiate to the point of sale.

Whether you're a buyer or seller, you view the ultimate sales transaction from a different vantage point. Oddly enough, both are trying to achieve the same end result—purchase of a product or service that will fulfill the needs of both the buyer and the seller. Remember that the key to a successful sale is in the negotiation. The better negotiator you are, the better your chances for a good purchase or sale, and both parties can walk away from the transaction feeling good about their decision.

Chapter 32 - Creating a Winning Presentation

> *"Success is the good fortune that comes from aspiration, desperation, perspiration and inspiration."*
>
> - Evan Esar

Your presentation must scream "Action!". It must be highly interesting or you will lose the attention of your audience. You must create an atmosphere that causes them to give you their undivided attention. If you can do this, your chances of closing the sale will increase dramatically. You must take control of the situation. You must set the stage.

When you go into a presentation, check out the situation before you begin. Are there any potential distractions? Any unnecessary background noise? Do whatever you can at the outset to create a calm, focused environment for your prospect to give you their full attention. In my experience, the way you start your presentation has a lot to do with the outcome.

Never give your customer a price too soon. Take your time in your presentation and build value in your product. Slow your customer down so that they understand you are going to take your time to show them all the features and benefits of your products. By building value first, you move your customer out of the realm of number shopping. Most salespeople are intimidated by demanding customers, and deliver their price too soon, thinking that if they don't give in, they'll lose the sale. Ultimately, however, they lose the value in the long run, because you are selling more than just a low-priced product.

Take control in your presentation by asking questions. This lowers your customer's guard up front. Build a repertoire of presentations so you have flexibility. You must read your prospect and tailor your presentation style for the type of person they are. It should be no more than five minutes long if possible. Its should point out the main reasons that the prospect should buy from you and not the competition. Always speak with conviction and confidence in your voice. At the end of your presentation, point out other products and features that could increase the value of the product or service in your prospect's mind. Try to find out what price the competition has given your customer. This will help you fix the price point. If you are being undersold by your competition, don't lose faith. You can still ultimately win the sale by pointing out things that that customer may not know. This will give them the impression that you are more knowledgeable than your competitor. Once you've identified a need and sold them on a solution, you'll win the sale. I've sold thousands of products – and won the sale - even when the customer had low-ball offers from my competition.

Ten Critical Keys

The sales presentation is your chance to show and tell, but it's not all show and tell. You also need to think strategically about the customer's buying process and their needs, your competitors' offerings and why your solution is best. Here are 10 keys to planning a delivering a winning sales presentation.

Find out in advance how much time you'll have. Have you ever had a key decision-maker leave in the middle of your presentation because he or she was out of time? You aren't holding the attention of a prospect who is looking at the clock! At the beginning of the call, ask how much time the prospect has set aside. Then adjust your presentation to take no more than 60 percent of the allotted time. Why only 60 percent? Because your prospect's decisions to act typically occur at the end of a meeting, so you want to allow enough time to resolve any remaining issues and reach an agreement.

Another question I ask at the beginning of every sales presentation is, "Since the last time we met, has anything changed?" If your competitor gave them a presentation yesterday you may have a few new hurdles to overcome. And the sooner you know what those hurdles are, the more time you have to plan a response.

The next question you want to ask is "Where are you in your decision process?" If they tell me they have scheduled presentations with three suppliers, and I'm the first presenter, I know the chances of them agreeing to a decision at the end of my presentation are virtually nonexistent. Why? You play the customer. Suppose you schedule appointments with three suppliers -- would you make a decision at the end of the first presentation? No, because it would take more time, energy and stress to cancel the appointments than it would to just go ahead with them.

Also, you wouldn't cancel them because comparison is necessary to recognize value. Recently one of my clients showed me his new sales brochure -- he was obviously very pleased with it. My immediate reaction was that it looked okay but it did not strike me one way or the other. Then I asked him to show me what he was using before -- and I KNEW how much better this brochure was than the last! It was the comparison that allowed me to recognize the improvement. Your customers need comparison too, to recognize your value. So if it happens that you're the first presenter, and the customer is still not ready to commit to the sale, don't panic. Instead, come up with a reason to come back and see them after their other presentations -- when they will likely be in a position to make a decision. Still, go ahead and ask for the sale after your presentation, because people buy from people they like. Just avoid overselling, because your customer may think you're trying to be pushy.

The fourth key to effective presentations -- try to be the last presenter. If I'm the final supplier to present, and I've shown why I'm their best choice, it's only reasonable to ask for a commitment to buy. In one of the largest sales opportunities I've ever worked on -- I was the third of three presenters to a committee of seven decision makers, the most senior of whom was the executive vice president. About 10 minutes before the conclusion of my presentation the phone rang – the VP's cab had arrived -- he had a plane to catch. As he stood up I said, "Before you leave, may I ask you one final question? He said, "Sure." I asked him, "Now that you've evaluated all the options, is there any reason why my solution is not your best option?"

He said, "Yep!" And out it came -- his final reservation. It was a concern that I was ready for -- I had anticipated that it would be a concern -- but I never got the chance to respond to it because his comment triggered a firestorm of conversation around the conference table. The VP missed his cab -- but several other decision- makers drove him to the airport so they could continue their discussion. A few weeks later I learned that, in the car, a lower-level decision-maker had resolved his concern -- and I won the sale! This example also points out that today, as much as 90 percent of the sale takes place when you're not there. So you've got to make sure that the prospects championing your cause have the tools to sell other decision-makers for you.

A good sales presentation starts with a quick review of the customers' goals and objectives. Then list on a flip chart each of the customer's buying criteria. This list of criteria is your outline for an effective sales presentation. Show how your solution meets and exceeds each decision factor.

Throughout your presentation, get reaction from your prospects. After demonstrating a capability you could ask, "How would this be an improvement?" or "How would this help?" Interactive presentations keep prospects more involved and interested.

Communicate all of your unique strengths. Today, it's not enough to show that you can meet your customer's needs. Your customer wants to know two things: can you do what we need done and how can you do it better than the other options we are considering? So, you must have some reasons why you're their best choice. And to ensure that my strengths are understood, I always prepare a flip chart titled "Why We're Your Best Choice." Here, I put at least three reasons why I am the customer's best choice. Many times I'll list seven or eight reasons. The more reasons you have, and the more compelling those reasons are -- the better your chances of winning the sale.

Use visuals in your presentations because a picture is worth a thousand words. Support your important ideas with a picture, show images on an overhead, flip chart, or laptop computer. Keep your visuals simple. One idea per image. Make it interesting, relevant and readable.

If your customer is not in a position to make a decision at the end of your presentation, schedule another appointment. Come up with a reason to get back in there.

Last, but not least, have fun and be yourself. If you want to persuade other people, you must connect with them on a personal level first. Think of John Madden, the football commentator. Madden is successful because he makes emotional contact by just being who he is. To put more impact in your sales presentations, connect with your prospects by just being YOU.

Chapter 33 - Dressing for Success

> **"The clothes make the man."**
>
> - Mark Twain

"What do you think this is, a circus?" Don't let this be your prospect's first reaction when you come to a sales appointment! They might not say it out loud, but if you're dressed like a clown, chances are that's what they'll think you are!

Let your appearance reflect your professionalism any time you're presenting your product. Remember, you are selling yourself just as much as your goods and services. You should be well dressed and clean shaven. Ladies, show as little skin as possible – provocative dress will only take the focus off of your presentation. Here are a few specific things you should avoid. Remember, you're not out to get attention for yourself. You want the prospect to be impressed with what you have to offer them.

Guys -

> No Loud Cologne
> No flashy jewelry
> No bright colors
> No ripped shirts or pants
> No sandals
> Clean or neat shave
> Well-groomed hair cut
> No offensive slogans on shirt

Ladies -

> No loud perfume
> No ripped or cut clothing
> No super tight clothing

If the prospect sees that you value your appearance, they will be more willing to take the time to listen to what you have to say. They will also be more willing to spend money with you as opposed to other reps who take pride in their appearance. Also, make sure you are comfortable in what you're wearing, because if you aren't, it will show!

Every business person sells either a service or a product, and the first thing that ever gets sold is you. Sales people who look good are more confident, more assertive and most importantly, more productive. Some industries (IT, entertainment and media) have a more casual dress code but in the sales industries you have to respect your clients and therefore dress accordingly. What you wear is one of your most visible credentials and if you take the time and effort with your appearance it will definitely contribute to your success. Regardless of the type of company you work for, you need to have your own 'personal brand' which is made up of the way you look, how you act and how you behave.

Chapter 34 - Knowledge + Value = Profit

> *"The secret of success in life is for a man to be ready for his opportunity when it comes."*
>
> - Earl of Beaconsfield

To build your numbers and your profits, you must see yourself as your customer's personal consultant. Keep in mind that you're the one with the knowledge to satisfy the need. Your clients should view you as the expert on your products and services. The knowledge you've amassed in your area is worth a price to your customer. The hours you've put into learning are hours they won't have to spend, because they have you as their consultant. When they have questions, they'll turn to you for your expertise. This works out to be a winning equation for you. The knowledge you've gained adds value to your service. The result is increased profit for your business.

Most of us have had experiences, both good and bad, with contractors. I was building a house once and had plumbing problems. After contacting several contractors to price shop, I chose one who began the work but didn't finish. A second contractor was able to finish the work but was unfamiliar with the parts left by the first contractor. Eventually I gave up shopping for price and opted for value. The problems were fixed on the same day. The bill I received was more than the first two contractors put together, but I was happy because the job done right.

Experience proves that price doesn't always equal value. Real value could save you thousands of dollars in the long run. This is the message you should convey powerfully to your customers. Of course your competition may be able to beat your price, but can they offer the value? You have the flexibility to even increase your prices as necessary if you sell your customers on the value you will provide.

I've taken many customers away from the competition by simply adding value to my product. Sometimes you don't have to do much. It may be as simple as giving them a callback when they need help. Commit to increasing your knowledge and value everyday and your profits will skyrocket.

Value is complex as there are many criteria on which people assess it. Customers may respond to factors like increased convenience or visual appeal. Here are some simple strategies to add value to your product:

Benefits: People perceive value in a product that is multi-purposed. Display a comprehensive list of benefits that solve a range of problems.

Testimonials: What better proof that your product offers value than customers raving about it! Choose credible sources and vary testimonials to cover the different benefits of your product.

Brand: Create and promote your brand. People perceive more value in a branded product such as 'Nike' or a seminar with the 'Guru of Guerrilla Marketing' than in an unknown brand or identity.

Packaging: Choose colors and type of package that make your product look more valuable.

Price: Sell your product at a higher price than your competitors. People usually associate higher-priced product with better quality.

Bonuses: Add bonus products with their retail recommended prices so customers can calculate the added value of your product.

Affiliate program: Offer a financial reward for referrals so people can make money from your product. From an expense, your product becomes a source of income.

Guarantees: A strong guarantee such as '100% satisfaction guarantee' increases the perceived value of your product. It eliminates the risk of potential psychological stress caused by post-purchase remorse or dissatisfaction.

Alliances: Publicize your association with a well-known personality or your professional organization. These affiliations increase your credibility and the perceived value of your product.

After-sales service: People perceive value in excellent customer support. Provide an online database of FAQs (Frequently Asked Questions) and contact details as samples of your commitment to after-sales service.

Let customers evaluate competing products and discover that you offer more VALUE.

Chapter 35 - An Atmosphere For Success

> *"To be a great champion you must believe you are the best. If you're not, pretend you are."*
>
> –Muhammad Ali

What's your motivation? You have to discover what this is so that you can capitalize on it to create an atmosphere for success. It could be a picture of a loved one, or a spiritual poem or saying. Whatever it is, you can use it to your advantage to gain positive energy that will push you forward. I post my goals near the shower where I will be sure to see them every day. I also hang motivational art around my office to keep the energy positive as possible. Your car is also a great place to enjoy uplifting, inspirational entertainment for your mind. Doing these things will keep your mind focused with sniper-like precision.

We've all heard that what we focus on determines the results we get in life. That makes sense. If you want something badly enough, and you focus all your energy on getting it, you'll very likely achieve it. Whereas if you don't focus on getting it, you won't.

But the currency metaphor takes this idea a bit further. It suggests that we even get the things we *don't* want if we think about them long enough.

So if you constantly think, "I don't want to be poor. I hate not having any money. I don't earn enough to buy the things I want. My job sucks."–if you *spend* most of your thoughts on the experience of being poor, that's what you get.

We all know someone who constantly complains about how unlucky they are, how nothing ever goes right for them. And when you look closely at their life, what do you notice? They're right. They *do* seem to have worse luck than the average person.

Consider the salesperson who's so worried about not making the sale that that's all he can think about. During his sales presentation, do you think he's relaxed or tense? Do you think he's more concerned with solving his prospect's problem or selling his product? How do you think he'll respond to his prospect's objections, empathetically or defensively?

Clearly, a tense and defensive salesperson who's aggressively pushing his product is not going to have the greatest chance of making the sale.

So, if thoughts are currency, and you buy whatever you think about, the importance of a positive mental focus becomes obvious. Imagine that each week when you got your paycheck you went out and bought everything you didn't want. That's ridiculous, right? So, be as frugal with your thoughts as you are with your cash.

Four Simple Ways to Make your Mental Focus More Positive:

Increase your awareness of when and how often your thoughts go negative. Get in the habit of asking yourself, "What am I focusing on right now, and is it positive or negative?"

If your focus is negative, replace it with its positive opposite. Instead of dwelling on the things that are missing in your life, focus on what you already have and what's possible in the future. Get in the habit of asking yourself, "What do I love about my life?"

Defend yourself fiercely against outside toxic negative influences. Stay away from complainers and blamers. Limit your exposure to the sensationalized and negative media. Get in the habit of asking yourself, "What's influencing my mental focus right now, and is it positive or negative?"

Surround yourself with positive influences (or simply pay more attention to the positive that's already around you). Associate frequently with people who lift your spirits and inspire you. Decorate your home and work space with pictures and colors that make you feel good. Play upbeat music that gives you energy. Get in the habit of asking yourself, "What can I do or focus on that will increase the quality of this experience?"

Chapter 36 – The Power of a Plan

> **"If you are failing to plan, you are planning to fail."**
> -Tariq Siddique

Your best strategy for time management is to plan your busy time during your least busy hours. I usually get up early in the morning before anyone has a chance to call me with an issue. This gives me good uninterrupted time to consider how I can best use my time that day. This will keep you focused on the important issues and lead to greater sales and more profit.

Whatever time of the day works best for you, use it to your full advantage to clear away concerns and details that eat at your energy. Take care of paperwork, answer e-mails and generally de-clutter your virtual desk.

There's an old saying, that goes like this: "If you want to make God laugh, tell him your plans." So, you may ask, why plan?

Most people think the purpose of planning is to achieve the specific results that they're planning for. And that seems to make a lot of sense. If you want a certain result, you create a plan to get it. So that must be why you plan, right?

But hasn't it been your experience that no matter how carefully you plan for something, your actual path to your goal is at least a little different than your plan?

If that's true, if things rarely go exactly according to plan, then that can't be the purpose of planning. Think of that as the motivation for planning—the result you want is what motivates you to plan, but it's not the purpose. So what is the purpose?

The primary purpose for creating a plan is so that when the unexpected happens—when something new comes up—you can refer to that plan to help you make the best choice possible.

The real value and advantage to having a plan is that it gives you the ability to adapt quickly to changing circumstances and unexpected events.

For example, you create a plan for the week. It includes all of your appointments and top priorities and tasks for the week. At 11 AM on Tuesday, your boss tells you to drop everything to prepare a report for her by the end of the day. Dealing with that task now becomes your new top priority.

Because you already had a plan for the week, you can make informed and intelligent choices quickly about what to postpone, what to reschedule, and what to delegate so that you can deal with your changing priorities. Your plan empowers you to deal with those changes.

Imagine you didn't have a plan for the week and your boss gave you that task. You'd be trying to juggle all of your existing appointments and priorities and tasks in your head as you dealt with this new emergency.

At best you'd feel stressed out. That new task would create a ripple effect in your brain as you tried to mentally make all of those adjustments.

At worst, your brain would shut down, mentally dropping everything but the new task. You'd start missing appointments, missing deadlines. Where's the power in that?

Understand that time is fixed—we all have 24 hours a day, no more and no less. Your power is not in how much time you have. Your power is in how effectively you choose to use your time. And planning enhances your power to choose by giving you the context you need to figure out what to do when things change.

So let me repeat: The primary purpose for creating a plan is so that when the unexpected happens, you have the information you need to make the best choices possible.

Chapter 37 - Do What you <u>Can</u>

> *"The man who removes a mountain begins by carrying away small stones."*
> - William Faulkner

Whether you realize it or not, you are a creature of habit. Unless you do shift work, you probably get up at the same time everyday, follow the same routine to wake up and get yourself ready for the day, drive the regular route to work, do the same things once you get to work, and take the same route home at the end of the day. Once there, you probably have dinner, watch television or read the newspaper, and follow some sort of routine once it's time to go to bed. You set the alarm for the same time and when it sounds the next day, you start the cycle over again.

Don't get me wrong. Routines can be good. They help us improve our productivity. They allow us to multi-task. They make us feel comfortable, safe, and secure. They reduce stress. Plus, when we have developed a great routine, we can often generate more business. However, the drawback is that they can be difficult to break away from.

When you become accustomed to a specific schedule, it can be easy to forget changes in it. For example, if you usually schedule your first client meeting after 9:30 it is very easy to miss a meeting that was recently scheduled at 8:30. I recently encountered two situations that relate to this.

The first was an appointment with my manicurist. For several years, she scheduled her appointments on the hour or half-hour. So when she booked my manicure at fifteen minutes after the hour, she forgot about it and was several minutes late.

The second was my fault. I normally meet with my trainer early in the morning, three days a week. I had to re-schedule one workout due to a business commitment and made my appointment for a later time on a different day. Unfortunately, I arrived at the gym at my usual time only to realize that I was several hours early. The change in the schedule messed up my routine.

As a sales professional, you need to recognize that routines can prevent you from achieving your full potential. However, if you persist at incorporating that new technique into your sales approach, it, too, will become part of your new routine. That's the great thing about the human spirit and brain, it is very adaptable. The most successful people in business and in sales know that changes to their routine will cause them some discomfort. But, they are also very aware that these changes will become more comfortable and part of their routine if they work at it long enough.

It can certainly be challenging to change your behavior and routine when you are used to making a certain number of calls every day, or meeting with a specific number of clients, customers, or prospects. When you have a specific daily routine, it is usually difficult to incorporate something new. Or, when you have developed the habit of selling in a particular manner, it is very stressful trying to change your approach. I see this in my sales training workshops all the time.

People can intrinsically grasp a new concept or principle but experience difficulty trying to actually implement it into the way they sell. That's why many sales training programs don't work; you can't expect to change your behavior or routine immediately. The key is to keep applying the concept even though it feels uncomfortable and foreign. In fact, in most cases, you will begin to feel comfortable with the concept immediately after you experience the greatest frustration and difficulty. Consider learning a new sport, hobby, or task.

At first the movements feel uncomfortable. Your moves are not smooth, accurate or natural. And this feeling usually persists for quite some time. However, just when you feel like giving up because it has become too difficult and frustrating, something clicks and the movements start to feel more natural. You have now progressed to the stage of being able to achieve results. The same process happens when you decide to try something different when selling.

Most sales people don't enjoy cold calling because they don't work at developing their skills long enough. They go through the motions of making their calls everyday but they don't focus on improving their skills, nor do they stick with it for the necessary period. People who do acquire the ability to effectively cold call have made enough calls to understand the dynamics, develop their skill at calling, and incorporate it into their routine. Routines are powerful. However, to get the most from them, you do need to change them regularly.

Your schedule can get pretty full if you are calling ten people a day, following up on leads and doing the work required. You have to make sure that the work you are providing is of the best quality possible, or you will lose the customer in the long run. It is also of primary importance that you schedule several "activity periods" per week.

An activity is anything you do that gives you touch points with your customers and with others in a network environment. Six to eight is a good number, which should include at least one networking meeting per week. You should also put a service organization into your schedule. It would be very easy to get out of balance with ten activities a week but if you include all the places where you meet with people then it is a little easier. Do not overcrowd your schedule as you also have to make time for the work.

Chapter 38 – No Turning Back

> *"The most essential factor is persistence - the determination never to allow your energy or enthusiasm to be dampened by the discouragement that must inevitably come."*
>
> -James Whitcomb Riley

If you listen to the experts, starting a small business seems to be right up there with shark-diving and base-jumping as a dangerous activity that's best avoided. Thousands of small businesses are started every year in the U.S., and according to some experts, 90 percent of them go the way of the graveyard within the first five years.

But although new business failure rates are high, you've decided to give it a shot anyway. Here's what you'll need to know to keep your business out of the statistical graveyard.

The exact failure rate for small businesses is a hotly contested topic in business circles. Some experts believe that publicized failure rates are highly exaggerated, while others stand by their claim that the businesses included in most failure rate estimations only represent the tip of the iceberg.

Even so, most business experts conform to a theory of "thirds": Of all the new business startups, 1/3 eventually turn a profit, 1/3 break even, and 1/3 never leave a negative earnings scenario. According to a study by the U.S. Small Business Association, only 2/3 of all small business startups survive the first two years and less than half make it to four years. With numbers like that, it's no wonder so many would-be entrepreneurs think twice before taking the plunge.

But needless to say, there are certain things you can do to increase the odds of success. You don't need an MBA to make your small business profitable - just guts, determination, and a little common sense advice.

Attitude

If you start your business with the attitude that it's probably going to fail, guess what - it probably will. The businesses that succeed are those that are founded with an attitude of success. For successful small business owners failure is not an option, and so they avoid people who live and breathe negativity. Instead, they stay positive and move full steam ahead toward reaching their goals.

Sacrifice

Starting a small business is not a comfortable or luxurious undertaking. It requires nothing less than a total commitment to make whatever sacrifices are necessary to succeed. The most successful small businesses make sacrifices early on and reap the benefits once the business has surpassed the startup phase.

Risk

Looking for a risk-free investment? If so, you'd be better off putting your money is a savings account and avoiding small business altogether. Small businesses are inherently risky ventures. Sometimes the risks pay off and sometimes they don't. But unless you are willing to take the risks in the first place, there is virtually no possibility that your business will ever succeed.

Planning

More often than not, the one thing that separates small business successes from small business failures is planning. With all of the resources available to small businesses these days, there is no excuse for not taking the time to create an executable business plan for your company. A good business plan is a roadmap that highlights the best routes to profitability and warns you of potential hazards along the way. If you don't have one, it's highly likely that you'll be lost - and out of business - in no time at all.

Chapter 39 - Planting Seeds

> *"Show class, have pride, and display character. If you do, winning takes care of itself."*
>
> - Paul Bryant

Every sales professional should think twice before changing their phone number or email address. Every time you give out your information, every time you hand someone your business card, you are sowing a seed. Have you ever gotten a call from a prospect you spoke to months or even years ago? You never know when someone will decide it's time to make a decision.

I've had sales calls from people who have seen ads I placed years ago. Every investment you make to get your name and business information out there could pay off. Think of it as sowing seeds. When a farmer scatters seeds on the ground, he never knows which ones will take root and sprout. He just does his job and sows the seed. Don't ever be discouraged if your advertising or marketing campaign doesn't seem to be paying off. Sales success doesn't come overnight. In marketing, just about everything you do will reap some form of reward at some time in the future.

Any time you've given a prospect the opportunity to see what you are offering and say yes or no to your marketing effort, you've planted a seed. Someone may take your card and stash it somewhere on their desk. Then months later when he's in the market for your product or service, it could catch his attention. Your "seed" has done its job and you haven't said a word!

Sales success demands that you get big results from minimal investments. Don't be afraid to borrow ideas from others' commercial success. Find ways to borrow your competition's ideas without infringing on their rights. Spend time on a regular basis to research the advertising concepts that are working, in sales publications, newspapers, and online. Watch for the ads that are continually running – these are the ones that are working.

Don't ever leave a sales appointment without getting your business card into your prospect's hand. Also keep one of theirs for your follow up. Take advantage of inexpensive means of conveying your sales message, like sending out emails with a powerful presentation attached to them. Think about it – your sales message could be traveling through cyberspace and selling for you while you're asleep!

I once came up with a winning presentation that was closing nine out of ten prospects that heard it. I thought to myself, "How can I get my sales force to get these kinds of numbers?" I came up with a flip chart that gave the presentation for them. All the reps had to do was flip the chart. By the next week, their sales volume was way up.

Remember the parable of the sower and the seed from the Bible? The farmer planted the seeds. Some fell on hard ground and didn't grow. Some took root and grew a little. Other seed fell on the good earth and grew and yielded an abundance of fruit. You are a planter. You must fine tune and deliver your message to everyone you can to reap the harvest of success.

Chapter 40 - Never Pre-Judge Leads

> *"Experience is a hard teacher because she gives the test first, the lesson afterward."*
> —Chinese Proverb

A good salesman knows he should never pre-judge a lead. This could be the deal that makes your sales goal. Treat all your leads the same. Give each one the attention required to turn it into a sale.

Once when I was out prospecting, I came upon a store that looked like it was run down. When I looked inside, however, I saw some well-dressed men selling merchandise. Even though it was the end of the day and I was tired, I thought, "I'll just step in for a minute and see what happens." It turned out the prospect there was looking for my particular service. He qualified and I made a huge commission off of the deal. It was an opportunity that I could easily have missed.

Any energy you spend pre-judging your leads is counterproductive. Always think positively. Negativity could rob you of the excitement of winning a new sale. This process will be full of ups and downs. When you fail to enjoy all the prospects that have been placed in your path, you'll lose the magic that comes with prospecting. Even if your prospect is a certain "no," giving them a presentation will sharpen your skills. If the prospect isn't ready yet, you can always ask them for referrals. Learn to see each time you get in front of a new prospect as a "win-win" situation.

Selling is all about the whys. There are some very important whys that you want answered and there are some very important whys your prospect wants answered. If you focus on these whys, selling will become a lot easier for you plus it will be easier for your prospects to buy from you.

So what are these whys and why are they so important?

When you are talking to a prospect the whys that you want answered are:

The real 'reason why' they want this problem solved or they want to obtain this outcome.

You want to find the 'reason why' because you need to discover the ultimate outcome they want. If you know the ultimate outcome they want, you will not only increase your chances of gaining a client but you will also probably make an even larger sale. Also, if you think about it, you need to know the ultimate outcome your prospect is looking for before you can propose the solution that is going to give them this ultimate outcome.

Let me clarify this with a very simple example. If someone wants to buy a drill, they are wanting to get an outcome which is the hole. If you go one step further and you find out the 'reason why' they want the hole, you will find the ultimate outcome. If they said they want holes so they can put up shelves, you could now focus the conversation on a solution which will give them the ultimate outcome they are looking for: shelves. You have now increased your chances of making a sale as you are now focusing on giving them what they really want: shelves. Plus by focusing on a solution that gives them shelves, you could probably include additional components and make an even larger sale.

Why they want this ultimate outcome NOW.

You want to find out why they want this ultimate outcome now as you need to know if there is a compelling reason to take action now. If there is no compelling reason to take action now, chances are high that they will not make a decision now. If there is no compelling reason you will probably be wasting your time, money and resources in pursuing a sale that is not going to happen now.

So just as you have whys you want answered so too does your prospect. The whys your prospect wants answered are:

Why should I buy this product or service?

Your prospect wants to know what's in it for me? If I buy your product or service? What problem does your product or service solve and what outcome is it going to deliver? What difference is your product or services going to make for me? Is there a justification for buying your product or service? Why is it important for me to buy your product or service now instead of later?

Why should I buy this product or service from you?

Once your prospect has made the decision that they want to buy a product or service like yours to solve a problem or achieve an outcome, they will probably also think they can buy this product or service from other companies as well. It is at this point they start asking themselves all sorts of questions about you. Are you capable of solving this problem and delivering the outcome? Will you do what you say you will do? Can I trust you? What risk am I exposing myself to if I buy from you? Will I get the outcome I want if I buy from you? Why should I buy from you instead of your competitors?

If you look at your sales conversations and all your steps in the sales process, they really are about finding out and answering these whys. In essence you want to find out why they want a problem solved now so you can know if they are really a prospect. In essence your prospect wants to know why they should even be interested in your products and services and if they are, why they should buy from you. Selling really is all about the whys.

Chapter 41 - Handling a Challenging Sales Call

> **"Though no one can go back and make a brand new start, anyone can start from now and make a brand new ending."**
> —Carl Bard

Let's face it. We all have those difficult customers to whom we are required to sell. From the demanding, abrasive buyer to the individual who never seems to make a buying decision, we encounter challenging people on a regular basis. Part of the reason this happens is due to the disconnect we have because of conflicting personalities. This article will look at the four key types of people and how to improve your results with each.

Direct Donna. Donna is very direct in her approach. She tends to be forceful and always wants to dominate or control the sales call. Her behavior is aggressive. She points at you while she talks, interrupts you to challenge you, and she seldom cares about hearing the details of your new product or service. Instead, she demands that you "cut to the chase" and "tell me the bottom line." Donna is very results-focused and goal-oriented and hates wasting time.

To achieve the best sales results with this individual you need to be more direct and assertive. Tell her at the beginning of the sales call or meeting that you know how busy she is and how valuable her time is. Tell her that you will "get right to the point" and focus your conversation on the results she will achieve by using you product or service. Resist the temptation to back down if she confronts you because you will lose her respect. To Donna, it is not personal, it's just business.

Lastly, be direct in asking for her business—you don't have to dance around this issue.

Talkative Tim. Tim is a gregarious and outgoing person but very ego-centric. He is often late for your meetings and his constant interruptions and long stories cause your sales calls to go beyond the scheduled time. He appears to be more concerned with listening to himself talk which is frustrating because you don't always get enough time to discuss your solution.

Relationships are very important to Talkative Tim so invest more time in social conversation. Even if you don't see the point in this, he will appreciate the gesture and will like you more. This person often makes buying decisions on intuition and how he feels about the sales person.

Be careful not to challenge Tim because he will feel rejected and when this happens he will "shut down" and become unresponsive. During your sales presentation, tell him how good your solution will make him look to others in the company or how his status or image will improve. In other words, appeal to his ego.

Steady Eddie. Soft-spoken, Eddie is a "nice" fellow who seems more focused on his team and coworkers than on his personal results. He is very quiet compared to some of your other prospects and can be difficult to read. But most frustrating is his reluctance to make a buying decision. Eddie's mantra seems to be "I'm still thinking about it but thanks for following up."

Structure and security is important to these people and it is difficult for Eddie to make changes. He often contemplates how the decision will affect other people within the organization. That means you need to slow down the sales process, demonstrate how your solution will benefit the team, and remove as much risk from the decision-making process as possible. Soften your voice and make sure your sales presentation flows in a logical manner. Use words like "fair" "logical" and "your team" in your presentation.

Analytical Alice. She reads every point and specification about your product or service and regardless of how much information you give Alice, she always wants more, including written guarantees and back up documentation. She is very difficult to read and it is extremely difficult to get her engaged in an open conversation because personal feelings and emotions do not enter the picture when Alice makes a decision.

Whenever possible, give Alice a written, bullet-point agenda of your meeting—beforehand. Ideally, email it to her a few days in advance so she can prepare herself. Make sure it is completely free of typos, spelling mistakes and punctuation errors. When you meet, follow the agenda in perfect order and if you make any type of claim, have supporting documentation available for her to read.

While the approach to use with each of these people may not make sense to you or seem completely rational, it is critical to recognize that how you naturally and instinctively sell may not be the best way to get results with someone else. Modifying your approach and style, even briefly, will help you better connect with your customers and prospects which means you will generate better sales results.

Chapter 42 – Maximizing Sales Performance

> *"The pessimist sees difficulty in every opportunity. The optimist sees opportunity in every difficulty."*
>
> —Winston Churchill

In essence, there are three levels of sales performance. The first is based on a simple formula; "pitch and pray." Once salespeople learn how to present the value of their solution, they feel confident and enthusiastic about pitching new customers over and over. What these salespeople don't know is how much more they could sell if they replaced their pitch with a meaningful support structure.

The second level of sales performance is based on the belief that process is progress. At this level, salespeople begin to learn more about the rational mind of the buyer. They begin to understand the core purchasing behaviors that govern a certain market or industry. After salespeople learn how their customers make their purchasing decisions, they may refine their sales process to more closely mirror the customer's buying psychology. This will improve overall sales, but Second-level salespeople enjoy higher levels of success, but the downside of process-focused selling is that as many as a third of all customers are not guided by rational decisions.

The third level of sales performance is collaborating with the client and co-creating new solutions. Reaching this level doesn't mean giving up pitching or following a process, it means exploring the irrational landscape within the client organization with the goal of creating new opportunities, larger budgets, greater relationships, and far greater sales.

This irrational landscape exists in every organization, because people don't know what they don't know. Level-three salespeople suspend their preoccupation with the sale and, when appropriate, suspend the need for following a process. They shift into a diagnostic mode in which they use their inner radar screen as their guide, with the ultimate goal of co-creating a new agenda with the prospect. Here are some of the tools level-three salespeople deploy:

Curiosity – that is open, inviting, casual, engaging, honest, collaborative, and almost playful.

Listening – that inspires trust and leads to an open exploration of goals, preferences, resistance, and apprehensions.

"Helicopter vision" – that provides a more detached view of where the client is located in relationship to his or her own environment and market.

Intuition – that allows the salesperson to sense the thoughts and impulses triggered in his or her mind while the client is talking. These hunches or gut feelings are often the precursor to significant discoveries. Level-three salespeople believe that their job is to awaken possibilities in other people and their companies.

While level-one salespeople use verbal eloquence as their sales tool, and level-two salespeople use a logical process as their road map, level-three salespeople use their inner capabilities as their guide. Instead of yielding to the impulse to pitch or control, they deploy their sensing qualities and suspend their preoccupation with success. They know that by letting go, they gain the trust of the customer, and by co-creating the business agenda, they often gain complete control over the customer's budget.

Ever wondered, what it took to become a top performer?

I used to wonder why I was struggling to get sales while my peers were sailing past me. I decided that I was going to find out by observing, questioning my peers and researching various tools and programs. This is what I found:

1. They come out of their comfort zone i.e. they are wiling to try things which most people are not until it becomes comfortable, like talking to strangers, making cold calls and going to networking events alone to meet new prospects.

2. They are committed to results. Commitment is doing the things you know you should do long after the mood you said it in has left you. They are committed to reach their daily targets, i.e. 160 cold calls, 3 appointments set, 1 new person to meet a day.

3. They are motivated. They set large specific goals like "I am going to earn $5,000 by September 31st. They break down their goals into daily actions so that it motivates them. They have pictures of what they are going to spend the money on plastered on a dream board or fridge.

4. They begin with the end in mind. They ask themselves the regular question; what would the more refined successful, accomplished version of me say to a prospect? What clothes would I wear? How would I act? And what would I do? By asking questions before taking actions, results in more effective actions. This brings them closer to being the future developed version of them.

5. They delay gratification. They discipline themselves by doing actions what successful people do so that they can they have what successful people have. Things like studying sales and successful sales people while other people are in the pub or watching television.

6. They expect positive results. They always expect the sale and focus on solutions to every situation. They understand that where attention goes energy flows. As a result they nearly always get a positive result because they are focused on it.

7. They are team players. They understand that they need to have great relationships with all resources and people, i.e. people in the back office, customer services and other areas because you never know when you need a favor to get a sale through.

8. They have enthusiasm. If you catch fire with enthusiasm people will come from miles to watch you burn. Become more passionate about

your company, products and your goals and this will show in your pocket.

9. They work harder. Successful people start cold calls early when most people are having breakfast or coffee. They are still calling prospects or finishing their paperwork long after others have gone home.

10. They take action daily. Successful people take action towards their goals every day - whether they feel like it or not. They know it creates a habit of action which translates into results. They make alterations to ensure that they get the desired results.

Chapter 43 - Creating Confidence

> *"If you can find a path with no obstacles, it probably doesn't lead anywhere."*
>
> —Frank A. Clark

What is the secret for successful sales? Is it low cost? Is it a famous brand name? Is the secret to successful sales to have the most features, at the best price, with the best quality or performance, before the competition? The secret to successful sales may surprise you.

The secret to successful sales is not the lowest price, the most features, the best quality, best performance, or to be ahead of the competition. The first ingredient to successful sales is trust.

Establishing trust is the most important element of successful sales. Without trust, how can the customer believe that you will deliver on the promise of a low price, best features, quality, or performance. The offer of a low price may be based on sacrificing quality or performance? The lure of advanced features may introduce unexpected defects, may be difficult to use, or may not be compatible with other devices. What good are the great features if they cannot be used? What happens to trust if there is a low cost in the beginning, followed by constant expenses to correct, upgrade, or fix problems in the product, software, process, or service? Deception and misrepresentation erode confidence, destroy trust, and create a barrier to sustainable sales.

If you cannot be trusted, then nothing that you offer has any real value. That is a powerful statement, and an important realization. If you cannot be trusted, then your promises cannot be believed. Promises may be in the form of commitments, pamphlets, brochures, presentations, and marketing materials. It is important to establish credibility and authenticity in marketing messaging as a basis for any and all marketing materials. If the source of the communication is untrustworthy, then the message is no different from the sales hype that comes from any other office. Trust and confidence must be established in marketing, and through the sales cycle, if it is to be believed in a contract.

How can you establish trust?

The first step to establish trust is to know what you have to offer. This applies to products, people, processes, software, and services. Whatever is offered by you, or your organization, must be clearly and precisely defined. It is quite likely that there are many benefits available from the product, process, or people. To be accurate and effective, identify the specific benefits from the perspective of your customers. Put aside the contemporary marketing idealism of creating benefit statements to justify purported benefits to justify differences, and focus with precision on the real value as identified through the eyes of your clients. Look inside yourself for a unique blend of talent, experience, and knowledge that can be contributed to support the goals and interests of your clients.

Use your skills and expertise to make your clients successful, and you will be amazed at how successful you will become in the process. Communicate the value of your offering with the same integrity that you would communicate your personal value. You have to be honest with yourself before you can be honest with anyone else.

The importance of being earnest is that you must be truly dedicated to the welfare of your customers. This not only means investing your personal expertise with the intent to support the success of your customers, but it also means the capacity to be honest when it is difficult to do so. Typically, the most difficult time to be honest with your customers is when you need to deliver news about an error, a failure, an accident, or a failure to perform according to expectation. It is important to be honest in communicating mistakes. If you can be trusted to acknowledge accidents, then accomplishments are that much more believable.

The ability to communicate honestly and effectively after the sale is just as important as the ability to acknowledge risk before the sale. Acknowledge risk, identify countermeasures and preventative measures to demonstrate your commitment to be a trusted advocate for your customers.

Some customers will not appreciate your integrity. Trust is not important to all customers, but it is important to the loyal ones. Some customers will make a decision based purely on price, with no respect to the importance of integrity or credibility. The customers who purchase from your competitor based purely on price will also be swayed by changes in price, which means that there is no loyalty to the competition either. To focus pursuit and acquisition of customers exclusively on price is to risk the sacrifice of profit, and to disrespect the customers who value loyalty. While it is necessary to be priced competitively, keep a healthy focus on investments in loyalty and integrity as the foundation for sustaining business. To live by the discount is to die by the discount, but mutual loyalty with customers can sustain and survive through even the most challenging circumstances.

Earn a reputation for being trustworthy with your communications and your actions. Demonstrate your commitment, and it will reinforce credibility. Focus on the success of your customers, and many of them will return the dedication with loyalty and referrals. Build a personal brand based on authenticity and integrity. Cultivate honesty and trust in the organization, and you will be amazed at how much easier it is to grow future sales with loyal customers.

Chapter 44 - Duplicating Success

> *"Vision without action is a daydream; action without vision is a nightmare."*
>
> —Japanese Proverb

In order to compete in today's business environment, your business simply must have a healthy customer referral program. Contrary to popular belief, customer referrals don't just happen. They require an intentional effort to get the right people talking about your company and your products.

With the a little know-how and a lot of hard work, you can put customer referrals to work in your business. Here are some tips to get you started.

Be selective

Not all of your clients and customers will be good prospects for referrals. Your job is to identify and cultivate the clients who have the potential to promote your business to the right people. You should be looking for clients who have expressed enthusiasm about your products and are well-connected with networks of people who are likely to be interested in what you have to offer.

Ask

Once you have identified clients who may be good candidates for referring your business to others, your next step is to ask them if they would be willing to make recommendations on your behalf. Some business owners find asking to be the most difficult part of the referral process. But the fact is that until you ask for them, you won't get the volume of referrals you want in your business. Period.

Educate

Asking for referrals is important. But it's also important to provide your clients with the selling tools they need to promote your products. This can be done any number of ways ranging from short e-mail announcements about special promotions to taking a key client out to lunch to educate him about the scope of your products and services. Be creative. But more importantly, keep your existing clients in the loop.

Create incentives

Everyone likes to feel special. One of the best things you can do for your business' referral program is to reward clients who successfully refer your products and services to other clients. Sometimes these rewards may come in the form of discounts. Sometimes they may come in the form of free merchandise or services. Whatever the reward, consistently reinforce the fact that you appreciate and value customers who are willing to help you promote your company.

Plan and track

Developing a marketing referral plan is probably the last thing on your mind. But if you are really interested in jumpstarting customer referrals, it should be the first. A marketing referral plan identifies your target customer base and establishes referral goals for a given time period. It also contains a mechanism to monitor how effective your referral system is working. (This could be as simple as asking customers how they heard about your company.) The result is a customer referral program that can easily be analyzed and adjusted to suit your needs and goals as a small business owner.

Requesting referrals from clients and prospects is critically important in sales. Referrals will strengthen your pipeline and establish credibility with prospects. You are significantly more likely to get a call back when you leave a voicemail stating that "So-and-so from XYZ Company suggested I call you about our solution."

Here are some tried and true techniques for getting referrals:

The Top Down Request: You can speed up the sales cycle with a top-down referral (with the decision maker referring to someone on their team). "I know you are not the person who would actively evaluate our solution but who on your team would be?" While you don't quite have "buy in", there is "approval" from management to look at your product.

The Narrow Down Request: It's easier to choose from 20 people than from the world so this approach narrows the choices. "Are there any other people within your organization who could benefit from our solution?"

Help Me Request: On a whole, people like to help, so when you pose an open ended question it usually works. "I was hoping you could help me, can you think of anyone (else) who could benefit from our solution?"

Thank You Request: Thanking the person before the referral makes them feel obligated to help. "If you could point me in the right direction, I would greatly appreciate it."

The Guilt Request: Believe me this one works. "I realize our solution does not seem to meet your requirements at this point in time, can you think of anyone that might benefit?"

The Good Friend Request: Here's another great way to request a referral. "Can you think of someone within your organization or industry, who should know about our solution?"

The "If You Were Me" Request: This places the person in your shoes and makes them stop and think about it. "If you were me, and you wanted to let people know about our solution, who would you call?"

Chapter 45 - Fortune in Follow-Up

> *"Life is a leap into the unknown. If you want a guarantee, buy a toaster."*
>
> —Bill Harris

How many times have you called a customer back and they said they already have the service that you were offering them last week?

Following up is an important aspect of closing a sale. Many businesses either neglect it or do not have an established plan to follow up. The first step is to have a means of reaching the customer, either through the Internet, by phone, or by mail. Therefore, you need to establish how you will get in contact with the customer and how you will gain specific contact information.

When following up, contact the customer with a reason that provides a step forward in the sales process. Don't call just to ask if they've made a purchasing decision. Such a follow-up not only puts customers on the spot but also assumes that they have all of the information they need to make a decision. Likewise, calling or emailing just to check in does not move the sale forward.

During the first meeting with a potential customer, find out what they want and what it would take to close the deal. Then, send them applicable information. If you have no new information, contact them with news of a special sale, for example. Your follow-up can relate to the additional information you sent them. Don't ask if they received it, but instead explain how it might benefit them. Use the new information to move the conversation forward.

Follow-ups demonstrate your determination to build relationships with your customers, and most significant sales are the end result of a relationship. You will still find a lot of disinterested parties, but a few potential buyers will appreciate the extra effort. These can become your best customers. In the long run, sales follow-ups are more cost-effective than chasing down new customers.

Did you know that 81% of all sales happens on or after the fifth contact? If you're a small business owner and you're only doing one or two follow-ups, imagine all the business you're losing. Not following up with your prospects and customers is the same as filling up your bathtub without first putting the stopper in the drain!

But don't be disheartened if you're among the 90% of business owners I talk to that don't do any follow up. The good news is you have ample room for profitable improvement. Consistent follow-up creates a predictable and profitable stream of prospects and customers that buy. Small businesses that capture leads and follow-up with them enjoy higher conversion rates and a higher percentage of referrals than those that don't.

After asking many small business owners the reason they don't follow up I often hear responses such as, "I don't have the sales staff to chase down all our leads", or "We're usually too busy to do a lot of follow up." These responses automatically set off red flags that tell me that they lack a systematic process for following up. The problem is not that they don't have the capacity to follow up with prospects, it's that they don't have the systems in place to do it.

What Does a Good Follow Up System Look Like?

A good follow up marketing system should have three attributes.

1. It should be systematic, meaning that the follow up process is done the same way every time.
2. It should generate consistent, predictable results.
3. It should require minimal physical interaction to make it run, meaning it should be able to run on autopilot.

Sounds like a dream come true for most small business owners doesn't it? Not only can it be done, it's being done every day. The secret to "follow-up marketing" is to make it automatic so that you don't have to lift a finger but the job still gets done. With today's technology it's simpler than ever. Automating your follow-up processes gives you more time to work "on" your business rather than "in" your business.

Three Types of Follow Ups

There are three types of people you should be following up with, suspects (people in your target marketplace), prospects (people who have responded to your marketing but have not purchased), and customers (people who have purchased something from you.) Each follow up message and offer will be different for each type of person. With suspects, you'll want to entice them to call you or visit your store or office. With prospects, you need to persuade them to make their first purchase. And with customers, you want to convince them to come back and do more business with you and give you referrals.

Obviously the hardest type of person to follow up with is a suspect because they haven't shown any interest yet in your product and you usually don't have their contact information. But that's not true with prospects and customers. You not only know who they are, but you should already have their contact information. And if you follow up with your customers with consistency you'll find that they will help you turn your suspects into prospects and prospects into customers.

Chapter 46 - Nurturing the Sale after the Sale

> *"Destiny is as destiny does. If you believe you have no control, then you have no control."*
> —Wes Roberts

After you close a sale, you may feel exhausted and think, "It's over." The truth is – it is NOT! Now you have to sell the customer on what you've sold them. They have trusted you as a salesperson, now they're watching your every move to make sure you can deliver what you've sold them. Lose them now, and it will be twice as hard to replace them with another sale.

Once you've sold a customer, your mission is to keep them as a client for life. Begin by sending a thank you card or email to let them know how much you appreciate their business. Develop all the strategies you can for staying in communication with them. It's worth it to invest a few dollars and hours to drip information on your customers letting them know you're still active in your business. This will build trust and confidence. When their friends are in need of your product or service, your name will be the first one they recommend. Your customers will become your "fan club" and you'll start to reap the residual rewards of your hard work. Offering customer incentives is a great way to insure your name gets out.

I once had a customer that referred several new customers to me. Since I hadn't been in this particular business very long, I had no idea of how to reward them for their help. Then I remembered that they loved ice cream. When I gave them the gift of their favorite ice cream, they were floored! The relationship blossomed into years of referrals and residual income. Aren't you ready to reap the residual effects of your hard work? Just a little after the sale care will pay off benefits that you don't even have to work for!

Ten Ways to Build Customer Loyalty

The key to a successful business is a steady customer base. After all, successful businesses typically see 80 percent of their business come from 20 percent of their customers. Too many businesses neglect this loyal customer base in pursuit of new customers. However, since the cost to attract new customers is significantly more than it is to maintain your relationship with existing ones, your efforts toward building customer loyalty will certainly pay off.

Here are ten ways to build customer loyalty:

Communicate. Whether it is an email newsletter, monthly flier, a reminder card for a tune up, or a holiday greeting card, reach out to your steady customers.

Customer Service. Go the extra distance and meet customer needs. Train the staff to do the same. Customers remember being treated well.

Employee Loyalty. Loyalty works from the top down. If you are loyal to your employees, they will feel positively about their jobs and pass that loyalty along to your customers.

Employee Training. Train employees in the manner that you want them to interact with customers. Empower employees to make decisions that benefit the customer.

Customer Incentives. Give customers a reason to return to your business. For instance, because children outgrow shoes quickly, the owner of a children's shoe store might offer a card that makes the tenth pair of shoes half price. Likewise, a dentist may give a free cleaning to anyone who has seen him regularly for five years.

Product Awareness. Know what your steady patrons purchase and keep these items in stock. Add other products and/or services that accompany or compliment the products that your regular customers buy regularly. And make sure that your staff understands everything they can about your products.

Reliability. If you say a purchase will arrive on Wednesday, deliver it on Wednesday. Be reliable. If something goes wrong, let customers know immediately and compensate them for their inconvenience.

Be Flexible. Try to solve customer problems or complaints to the best of your ability. Excuses like "That's our policy," will lose more customers faster than setting your store on fire!

People over Technology. The harder it is for a customer to speak to a human being when he or she has a problem, the less likely it is that you will see that customer again.

Know Their Names. Remember the theme song to the television show Cheers? Get to know the names of regular customers or at least recognize their faces.

I've personally witnessed both experienced salespeople and novices losing opportunities by not effectively asking for the close. You should practice asking for the sale in the mirror, so that when the time comes, you sound bold and confident to your prospect.

We all can use a new sales technique to sharpen up our sales strategy from time to time. Changing your strategy can make the sales more interesting – you won't sound so much like you're repeating a memorized script. I have used and taught this technique. It is very appropriate for retail sales, but it can be altered to work in other types of sales situations. Using this technique will help you determine your customer's buying temperature and will often surprisingly be the catalyst for the close.

Sometimes when we are engaged in a sale, we find that even though we have gone through the sales presentation efficiently, have been thorough in answering all objections and have even narrowed down the make, model or color that your prospect wants, the customer is still not making that buying decision. In other words, we just can't seem to close the sale. It may be that your customer is hesitating for some unknown reason. It could be as simple as that they were planning to go to dinner after talking to you and never intended to purchase right away, or perhaps even that they wanted to use a credit card that they left at home. This is the type of scenario in which you can very effectively use what I call the "Box-Step" sales strategy.

As soon as you have detected that your customer is waffling or stalling on making a buying decision, very politely step away from the customer and towards where ever it is that you keep your product inventory. It could be a stock room, a listing in your manager's office, or an adjacent building -- it doesn't matter, just take a step or two in that direction, then turn back to your customer and say, "Mr. Customer, I'm going to go check my inventory for you (pause)...if I have one in a box (or in stock) should I bring it up for you?" It has been my experience that if you have done everything else right up to this point, your customer will say, "OK -- sure!" If they are agreeable, then you can assume the purchase. Go ahead and bring the item up and write up your sale. It is very rare that you will bring the item up and the customer decides they don't want it. Congratulations -- you made the sale!

However, it may also happen that after you've asked them if you can bring it up, that your customer will tell you "no thanks". If this happens, then do not go to check your inventory, but instead turn and step back towards your customer and continue with where ever you were in the sale. In doing the "Box-Step" sales strategy, now you know how hot or cool your customer is to a decision to buy. Once you have stepped back to them and returned to the sale, you may discover that there was a detail that you missed. If so, resolve the issue and try the "Box-Step" strategy once again and see what happens. Often you will get a "yes" the second time around!

Chapter 47 - When Everything Goes Wrong

> *"Far better is it to dare mighty things, to win glorious triumphs - even though checkered by failure - than to rank with those poor spirits who neither enjoy much nor suffer much, because they live in a gray twilight that knows not victory nor defeat."*
> —Theodore Roosevelt

Yes, you and I both know that when life gives us lemons, we should make lemonade. But when it comes down to the nitty gritty, just how do you get through those unexpected, difficult situations?

Chances are you spend more time worrying about things that might possibly go wrong which never actually do. In other cases, we have absolutely no control over the events that befall us. What you need most for the real challenges is a child-like imagination. All of us become a little jaded as we grow older. Our childlike optimism gives way to cynicism and pessimism. Once you've reviewed your reasons and tapped into the future to see yourself accomplishing your goal, you'll have the energy to get through your present circumstances.

When disaster strikes, mentally take yourself out of your normal surroundings and put yourself where you want to be. Your circumstances may feel like you're walking through freezing harsh winter weather, but to get through it, imagine yourself out on the beach relaxing and getting a tan. Imagine looking out at the waves and pressing the cool sand between your toes. Feel refreshed? Although this is just an example, in order to get through a challenging experience you must practice visualizing yourself where you want to be. It may be a degree to help you start a new career. It may be a sacrifice you're making to later spend more time with your family. Whatever your reason, think of the end result in order to get the energy you need to get through it today.

You must learn to get through the rainy days in order to get to the better days. You can't stop in the middle of the race just because you stumble once, you must continue until the race is finished. Once I learned how to use the power of tapping into the future, I was able to achieve many of the goals I once thought were almost unreachable. On difficult days you're going to want to stay in that warm bed. Use these empowerment strategies to get yourself out to tackle what's frustrating you.

Visualization

One of the easiest things you can do to bring more success to your life in any area is to visualize it. Star athletes use visualization all the time to improve their performances so why shouldn't you use it to improve your life performance?

Visualizing success means creating clear pictures in your mind of having already achieved your goals. A few reasons visualizing success works are because it re-programs your brain to create new solutions for achieving your goals, it helps you see ideas that you may have been ignoring, and it relaxes and calms your body. Also, if you believe in the law of attraction, visualization helps attract the things you want to achieve into your life.

Here are six steps for applying visualization to bring more success into your life:

1) Decide on a specific goal you want to achieve such as a better relationship with someone, a new house, successful mornings with your kids, or the amount money you want in the bank. (When you are just starting out, pick a goal that you consider realistic. As you get better at visualization, you should add goals that are bigger challenges or are well beyond your comfort zone.)

2) Close your eyes and imagine yourself succeeding at that goal - see it as already complete.

3) Make the pictures in your mind as clear and complete as possible with vivid details. For example: What color is your new house? What does each room look like? What are you doing in the house? What sounds do you hear?

4) Feel what it feels like to be successful at that goal. Are you relaxed, happy, proud? Also, see if you can imagine a sense of peace that you might feel inside at having achieved your goal.

5) Try to do these steps at least twice a day for 10 minutes if possible - first thing when you wake up and again right before you fall asleep. If you are feeling overly stressed about a goal or decision, take a few minutes to visualize your success at that situation several times a day. This will help your body feel less stressed about it.

6) Visualization helpers - some people find it helpful to collect pictures to create "vision boards" or "goal books" where they paste or draw pictures that symbolize what they're trying to achieve. Also, you can keep a small notebook for writing down ideas of success as they come to you.

Visualization is a powerful tool that your mind uses all the time - maybe without you even being aware of it. Often when people are not succeeding at something, it's because they are habitually and perhaps unconsciously visualizing failure, pain, and negative situations. If you want to succeed , then take control of the images in your mind and use these six steps to visualize your personal version of success!

Chapter 48 - Knowing Your Competition

> "A coward gets scared and quits.
> A hero gets scared, but still goes on."
> -Unknown

It's absolutely vital to know your competition in order to sell your products to their best advantage. It's advisable to keep an eye on them at all times, since knowing who they are and what they're offering can mean you are much better placed to stand out and maximize your sales.

It's arguably unprofessional to criticize your competition when selling, but you can certainly play it to your advantage if you have a clear idea of their weaknesses. For this reason, if it is possible to get information from the customers about previous experiences with the competition, it could be very valuable.

It is also important to know if there are any new entrants to the market to ensure you retain your unique selling proposition (USP). If you have a good grasp of your industry, you're likely to know about that if someone comes along with something new to offer. However, you'll still need to use your Internet research and your contacts as well.

Don't just learn about the competition's product and pricing however. Whatever you use to sell your offering is important – the level of customer service, how it is sold, any customer loyalty devices, for example. And it also useful to know about the company itself – age, size, number of staff, even their accounts which are accessible at Companies House. Ask them for brochures, price lists, or any other marketing products.

From an entrepreneur's point of view, if it turns out that your competition is making more sales than you with good reason, you know things need to be changed. From the salesperson's point of view, there's no better way of finding out how to make your offering irresistibly different and convincing than knowing you're better than the competitors. Of course, this is what makes competition a healthy thing – driving you to be the best you can be.

Chapter 49 - Going Toe to Toe with the Competition

> *"The dictionary is the only place where success comes before work."*
>
> -Mark Twain

For anyone trying to grow a business, one of the first tasks is to map the competitive landscape. With a good understanding of your competition, you'll be able to spot and exploit opportunities as they develop. These points should help you draw and refine your map, beginning with your earliest efforts to plan your new venture and continuing for as long as you stay in business.

Be a customer. Bring a notepad and pencil to competing establishments and ask a lot of questions. Testing a firm's ability to serve you will reveal much about their business. And don't just pretend to shop from competitors. Buy something. It's the only way to gain first-hand experience with the company's products and services.

Find out as much as you can about the people who run competing businesses. Where did they go to school? Where have they worked? How long have they been in the business? What are their strengths and weaknesses? This information can help you anticipate your competition's moves. For example, a local, life-long farmer will run an Indiana seed company very differently than will a young MBA.

Buy stock in your competitors. If you're competing against a publicly traded firm, consider buying a few shares of its stock. That way you'll receive regular updates on the firm's financial results and business strategies.

Talk to your competitors' customers. Why do they buy from your competitors? Is it because of the quality of the product or service, the price, the location, or the customer support? What do they dislike about the company? What do they wish that company would provide? Why don't they buy from you?

Use the Internet. Online services such as Dow Jones Interactive allow you to search through thousands of publications for information about your competitors, especially if they include large companies. Searches are free, but you'll have to pay a fee for articles on Dow Jones or for a monthly subscription. You also can learn a great deal about competing businesses simply by going to their web sites.

Check public filings. As an entrepreneur, you already know that companies must disclose information to government agencies. Such disclosures are required to undertake public offerings, receive building permits, register for patents or trademarks and so on. Many of those filings are public record and contain information about the company's goals, strategies, and technologies.

Get to know local librarians. Many are expert researchers and can save you a great deal of time and effort. Your library also will have local publications that may have information on competitors in your area.

Attend industry conferences and trade shows. Your competitors' representatives will be pounding their chests about their firms' products or services. Take advantage of the opportunity to familiarize yourself with their product offerings and strategies, and how they sell themselves.

Assess the competition's goals. A competitor trying to increase its market share might lower prices; a firm attempting to increase profits may cut costs; and a business that wants to accelerate sales growth might kick off a marketing campaign. If you know your competitors' goals, you'll be better able to anticipate their strategies.

Be aware of the potential for new competition. These days, the competitive landscape can change faster than Net-stock valuations. A national chain may not have entered your region yet — but what if it does? Likewise, companies that don't currently compete with yours might shift their focus and put themselves against your firm.

Don't delegate the job of keeping up with competitors. You might appoint someone to work with you on the task, doing research and the like. But as the entrepreneur, you're in the best position to appreciate and act upon information about your competitors.

Define the competitive landscape broadly. Your competition includes anything that could draw customers away from your business. For example, movie theaters compete not only with other cinemas, but also with restaurants, live music venues, theater — even cable TV, video rentals, and video games.

Chapter 50 – Closing the Deal

> *"Success seems to be largely a matter of hanging on*
>
> *after others have let go."*
>
> -William Feather

Can you close a sale in just seven seconds? You can do it faster if you use a sales technique to make a great first impression. Seven seconds is the average length of time you have to make a first impression. If your first impression is not good you won' t get another chance with that potential client. Make a great first impression and the client is likely to take your product seriously.

Whether your initial meeting is face-to-face, over the phone or via the Internet, you do not have time to waste. It pays for you to understand the sales technique of how people make their first judgment and what you can do to control the results.

Learn the Non-verbal Sales Technique: When you meet someone face-to-face, 93% of how you are judged is based on non-verbal data - your appearance and your body language. Only 7% is influenced by the words that you speak. A good sales technique is to remember people do judge a book by its cover. When your initial encounter is over the phone, 70% of how you are perceived is based on your tone of voice and 30% on your words. It's not what you say - it's the way that you say it.

Choose Your First 12 Words: Although research shows words make up a mere 7% of what people think of you in a one-on-one encounter, don't leave them to chance. Express some form of thank you when you meet the client. Perhaps, it is "Thank you for taking your time to see me today" or "Thank you for joining me for lunch." Clients appreciate you when you appreciate them.

Use Their Name Immediately: Another forgotten sales technique is to remember there is no sweeter sound than that of our own name. When you use the client 's name in conversation within your first twelve words and the first seven seconds, you are sending a message that you value that person and are focused on him. Nothing gets other people's attention as effectively as calling them by name.

Pay Attention to Your Hair: Your clients will. In fact, they will notice your hair and face first. Putting off that much-needed haircut or color job might cost you the deal. Don't let a bad hair day cost you the connection.

Shiny Shoes Sales Technique: People will look from your face to your feet. If your shoes aren't well maintained, the client will question whether you pay attention to other details. Shoes should be polished as your sales technique. They may be the last thing you put on before you walk out the door, but they are often the first thing your client notices.

Walk Fast: A faster walker can be perceived as important and energetic - just the kind of person your clients want to do business with. Pick up the pace and walk with purpose if you want to impress.

Chapter 51 - Fighting Fear and Doubt

> *"Don't just give up trying to do what you really want to do.*
> *Where there is love and inspiration, I don't think you can go*
> *wrong."*
>
> -Ella Fitzgerald

I'll always remember the first sales course I ever attended and the definition of selling that was drummed into my brain: "Selling is the art of creating a desire in the mind of a buyer and satisfying that desire so that buyer and seller benefit."

Now that may seem a bit old-fashioned for many of today's salespeople, but I believe the principle still holds true, particularly if you're attempting to persuade another person, be it a member of our team, a colleague or a customer. If you're going to persuade someone to change their behavior, their viewpoint, their attitude, any other aspect of their business or personal life, then you're talking about changing a mindset.

For anyone to change their mindset, then they need to anticipate the benefits that will outweigh their present circumstances or situation. If you're the person doing the persuading, then you need the following skills, qualities and characteristics which make you believable and credible.

Belief - Successful persuaders believe in themselves and what they're talking about. After all, if you don't believe in what you're saying, how do you expect anyone else to?

Enthusiasm - I've known people who totally believe in what they're saying but fail to communicate with any enthusiasm or passion. If you want to persuade someone, you'd better find a way to get enthusiastic about it.

Knowledge - you must know what you're talking about, so make sure you have all the information, facts, figures and statistics to make your case.

Empathy - Put yourself in the other person's shoes. What do you think is important to them? Consider carefully why they should accept what you're saying. If someone is frightened of flying, then there's no point in telling them not to be silly and to stop behaving like a baby. You need to think about how you might feel in these circumstances and what might persuade you to change your mind; you need to outweigh the fear with benefits relevant to the individual.

Persistence - if you want to persuade someone, don't give up on the first "no" or rejection of what you say. Persist and persist - but do it nicely! People wont necessarily react in a negative way to your persistence when they realize you really believe what you're saying. There's a fine line between being persistent and being a nuisance. Watch the other person's reactions and if it looks like you're persisting too much - stop!

Energy - put energy into all your interactions with other people. Energy fuels enthusiasm; we are persuaded by people with energy. Many TV presenters use their energy to sell us their ideas. Think of the celebrity chefs on TV persuading us to produce fabulous meals or other presenters who get us all excited about remodeling our homes or gardens.

Consistency - Everything you do or say is important, everything counts. If you want to be a powerful persuader then you must be consistent. If you're trying to persuade someone to keep their promises, then you must always keep yours. If you say - "I'll phone you back in ten minutes" then phone them back in nine minutes.

To be a powerful persuader you need many skills, qualities and characteristics. Even with them all in place, there is still no guarantee of success. However, people are more likely to be persuaded by people they trust, they like and have a good relationship with.

Chapter 52 - Creating a System

> *"Success usuallly comes to those who are too busy to be looking for it."*
>
> -Henry David Thoreau

Creating a system for the delivery of your sales presentation is critical to your sales success. If you know what works, don't change it. For example, if you are new to your product and you find that many of your customers ask you the same question, then take the initiative to integrate that information into your presentation. By bringing it up first, you will save time and get to the closing process sooner.

Your presentation should highlight the key features and benefits of your product or service. I prefer to limit these highlights to the five most important features. Depending on your sales success with these highlights, you may change or reorganize what you emphasize.

By creating a system, you will do what McDonald's did to the fast food business. You will replicate your winning sales strategy over and over again to your greatest advantage. When you've got it working, you won't need to change things each time. Use visuals like a flip chart that lists the highlighted features. Get yourself a sales force so you can be selling in many places at the same time. You will leverage your profits immediately.

Stay on the alert for even more ways you can reach greater numbers of customers with your presentation. Deliver it on your website so your product will sell even while you're asleep. Download your presentation to a DVD that you can give to customers if they aren't available for a personal appointment. Once your systematic presentation is solid, you will already know what questions your client will ask, and it will be smooth sailing all the way to the closing table.

Speaking broadly, you can think of every sale as having four distinct phases. These phases sometimes blur into one another, or course, as the interaction between two or more individuals proceeds. But in general, the phases can be described as follows:

Research. Sales success begins with an understanding of the customer's unique situation, needs and ability to buy. The more a sales person can understand the customer, the better the chance for successfully completing a sale.

For example, when selling equipment, researching a customer's needs might include finding out about:

> The equipment the customer currently has
> Why the equipment needs to be replaced or added to
> Problems with the current equipment
> Specific future uses for additional equipment purchased
> Problems that need to be solved by a purchase
> Volume or quantity the new equipment will be required to handle
> Funds available for purchase

When these factors and others have been analyzed, the next step is to determine how the products the salesperson has available will meet these needs. A key element in this step is to become aware of differences in price and features between the equipment the salesperson can offer and what the competition has available.

The Presentation. In this phase, the salesperson meets with the prospective customer to discuss everything determined in phase 1. The more completely and accurately the salesperson can show why his or her company's products address all the customer's needs, the more compelling the presentation will be.

The presentation phase consists of describing how the customer's needs will be met, and answering questions (objections) put forth by the customer. Every question or objection should be thought of as an opportunity to demonstrate how the products offered will fill a need, solve a problem, increase profitability, speed up work, etc.

The Close. Volumes have been written about closing techniques. Most successful sales veterans continually study these techniques, perfecting their style and ability.

Ideally, the closing phase is a natural extension of the presentation phase (which of course is a natural extension of the research phase). When all questions and objections have been addressed, the salesperson needs to say or do something that finalizes the sale. In other words, something needs to be done so that the customer can formally end his or her search for what will solve the needs or problems under consideration.

Closing techniques include:

> Assuming the Sale ("We'll start delivery on that right away, if you'll just sign right here.")
> Closing with a Choice ("Do you want the 100 horsepower or the 125 horsepower model?")
> Asking the customer to take some action that implies acceptance ("Sign right here and we'll start arranging delivery.")

These and dozens of other closing techniques are proven ways to allow a customer to acknowledge that the sale has been finalized.

Post-sale Activities. After a sale has been completed, a salesperson needs to immediately focus on two things:

1. After-sale services, such as timely delivery, installation, employee training on new equipment, etc. The better this post-sales aspect is handled, the more likely a customer will be to make repeat sales.

2. Minimizing buyer remorse. It's natural for customers to temporarily regret or question their purchasing decisions. They may ask themselves: Did I pay too much? Could I have gotten

something that would have been better for my purposes? What if this doesn't work and I look foolish? By realizing that a customer might experience this phase (and might even cancel the sale because of it), a salesperson should address the problem before it grows stronger. Reiterate the wisdom of the purchase, how the purchase will meet needs and solve problems, and how the purchase 'fits the bill' and will make the buyer look good.

Every sale has some element of these four phases. Corporate sales may allow a salesperson to fully engage in all phases (extensively researching, having a face-to-face presentation with decision makers, using closing techniques and following up with post-sales activities).

Direct mail and print ad sales also involve each of the four phases described. The research phase is carried out by locating the most likely target markets (using appropriate mailing lists or types of magazines, for example), writing an ad copy that demonstrates how the product or service being sold will solve a problem or address a need, writing a "call to action" that encourages people to mail a check or call in for a credit-card purchase, and following up sales with excellent service that solidifies the sale, encourages future sales and minimizes buyer remorse.

Chapter 53 - Never Give Up!

> **"It takes 20 years to make an overnight success."**
>
> - Eddie Cantor

The secret to success is sticking to your goal no matter what. Don't give up before you make it to the top. One of the true measurements of success is time. If you've invested a small amount of income into your venture, it's easy to stop one day and say I'm going to do something else because I don't see any immediate results. Don't let the small investment detour you from sticking to it.

When I started to become successful it was only when I decided to stick to it. Even if it's something that you don't like, you can look at it as a stepping stone until you find something better. I've learned that hard work will never let you down. It will always lead you down the path to find what you need. Remember, this is a journey that you are embarking upon. There are going to be ups and downs and you must get through them all if you want to be the rewarded. There are no short cuts to success, if there were, I'm sure it would probably be on sale at your local Wal-Mart and more people would have the health they want, and the success they want, and fulfill all the dreams they desired.

You see success isn't bought, it's earned. You can never be successful if you're always moving from one thing to the other all the time. As soon as you start one thing, someone's going to tell you how much better something else is and how much more you can earn. Don't give in to the urge, give it a chance to work for you. In any business you have to diligently work every day to make it a success. You work hard on that job, why not do it for yourself. Listen to motivational CDs and material that inspires your mind. You should make you car your motivational listening room. It's easy to get discouraged early in the game because of the challenges that you have to go through to succeed. Everyone gets discouraged sometimes, so you must prepare for negativity by having that inspiration stored in your brain. Just as the camel keeps water stored for the long trip in the desert because they don't know when they will have an opportunity to drink. I think that's why God made them that way because their environment is hot and dry. He didn't want them to die of not having enough water when they needed it most. The same goes in your working environment. You should store up some positive encouragement for your mind. I never listen to the radio until the end of the day. Sure I want to listen to my favorite station, but with all the opinions and negativity that it puts into your mind, it can end up being very costly. I am constantly changing the motivation CDs in my CD deck and absorbing the messages to help me handle the down times, like when my prospect is not on time, or when I think I've got a deal in the bag and then my client puts me off for another month, or when the customer wants to low ball your price and you have to have the energy to get their thinking up to par.

It takes a lot of energy to sell, so your mind must be prepared in advance for discouragement. Pat yourself on the back, because you're taking a road less traveled. If you give up now, you will never know the person you could have become. You will always say to yourself, what if or If I would have stuck to it where would I be now. Sure sometime along the way you'll have to review the results and channel your focus to more productive directions. Review your results, Start again but never give up.

Chapter 54 - The Day you Succeed

> *"People rarely succeed unless they have fun in what they are doing."*
>
> - Dale Carnegie

The attitude of success is a completely learned behavior. It is a frame of mind and a determination that lets you achieve anything you want, since you know that you will create the opportunity and then make it occur.

You may not necessarily know how you will create the opportunity, you just know that you have to achieve something positive and you have the ability to learn whatever it takes to acquire the attitude of success. With this in mind, you need only to identify what you really want to learn about, and then gather the information needed to get it.

Preparation, planning, modern time management and skills are keys to success in all our life activities. So, If you want to build a business on a strong basis, you'll need to take the time needed to learn, prepare and plan properly. Always be willing to learn more about your pursuit. Before jumping into online battle, there are several things you will want to consider.

What does starting a business involve? What should you expect? And, are you suited to this lifestyle? As with any employment decision, the proper skills, plan, time and research should be spent to make sure you're on the right track.

Your knowledge, your skills, your service or product quality, will not help you enough if you don't have the right attitude. Many people fail in their business and the major reason of their failures is due to inadequate attitude. This brings me to an old statement "Your Attitude determines your Altitude," pretty much says it all!

It is a sad aspect of life that not everyone will be successful. In the world we live in, there are winners and losers. Most people want to be in the group of winners but unfortunately many remain where they stand and the main reason is the lack of skills and determination.

Success doesn't come free or cheap. You have to pay for it. The price is not monetary but it is expressed in manners of time and effort, these being precious details that you can't receive back once you gave them away.

Success in your business is your challenge to achieve. Generally speaking, to be successful you have to work hard, and continually educate yourself about your pursuit. Often you have to try many times until you truly reach success.

Not being successful is simple! You make all the wrong choices, you work without ethics, the lack of responsibility and of education is almost everything. Although it is not as obvious, lack of success is also a choice - a choice that you can make on the first try.

Everyone thinking of starting a work at home business needs to be prepared to move beyond conventional approaches. One of the most crucial factors in your business success is your ATTITUDE. Understanding the attitude of success and what you should do to be successful are your keys to being able to reach your goals.

Here Are Some Practical Tips On How To Achieve Success:

Build up a purpose in life, create a plan and go on living by it.

Alter your behavior and become more stable and disciplined.

Always read, always learn and always communicate.

Think and act fast when faced with an opportunity. If you see what you really want don't let any chances pass you by. This one might just be the last you will get.

Give up bad habits and keep the good ones. Eat well and regularly, get enough sleep, go to a gym or just go jogging.- Give up watching so much television, or playing games.

Try to work more in the shortest possible period of time.

Keep your sense of humor but don't become rude.

Cherish everything you have and get.

Find out more, be responsible, learn about control and always stay informed.

The attitude of success is a learnable skill. You can learn to succeed at anything. You can become more focused by using effective learning techniques. Your key to success is finding out what works for you. Anyone and everyone can have success but you just need to grab it for yourself in leaps or small steps.

Chapter 55 - Preparing for Success

> *"We would accomplish many more things if we did not think of them as impossible."*
>
> *- C. Malesherbes*

So here you are, face to face with a customer you've been trying to close a sale with for months, and you've finally gotten them to the point that they're ready to sign on the bottom line. The time is right, your energy is higher than ever before – you reach for your notebook and you realize you don't have an application! Trying to recover, you say "Let me check my car . . . " but it doesn't take long for you to figure out that there's no application in your car.

Ideas are racing through your head – how can I get that application so I can close the deal? The customer has been waiting for several minutes for you to come back, but realizing that the line is getting long, they politely tell you to come back next week when they will have more time to speak to you. The excitement you felt just a little while ago skyrockets out of the sky and crashes on the ground. You've lost today's opportunity.

Preparation is where you meet success. You should always take the time to make sure you have all the material you need to fight and win. A soldier wouldn't go to war with only a knife. For battle, he is armed with the best high-tech machinery available to ensure his success.

Speaking with Ease

For most of us in sales, words are our most powerful weapon. How well we use them – our public speaking skills – can really make or break a presentation.

The words public speaking strikes fear in the minds of otherwise competent and confident people. Master the art of public speaking for greater success. There are many ways to increase business exposure so why bother to overcome your speaking jitters? Stepping up to the podium not only positions you as an expert in your area of business but provides effortless referrals and improved sales opportunities.

Presenting a non-sales informative speech warms up your target market and builds trust. Unlike endless cold calls the people you present to and follow up with are more receptive to listening to your offering of products and services.

Overcome your fears of public speaking and boost your business with these 7 tips to master the art of public speaking:

7 Tips to Master the Art of Public Speaking

Start Small: If you're new to the world of speaking, start small. Find a few friends and family to practice on. Begin by speaking to smaller groups and build up from there.

In my business speaking career, I speak to groups of 30 to 3,000. One discovery I made is the size of the audience makes no difference. If you know your topic, you're pre-speaking fears will quickly evaporate.

Prepare: Nothing helps ease the speaking fears than knowing your material. The ability to connect with your audience comes from having the confidence you won't get lost during your delivery. Rehearse several times before the big talk. Time your presentation and always have back up material in case time is left over.

Don't Memorize: Mastering the art of public speaking comes not from memorizing word for word your entire speech. The real pros know their material by remembering key points and prompts on sub topics and examples to cover.

Avoid Bullets: The majority of business presentations and speeches are boring monologues filled with endless PowerPoint slides and bullet points. Trash the PowerPoint presentation and make your material the focal point of the talk. If you do use PowerPoint, take the approach of using visuals that quickly convey your message.

Reduce Stress: The most fearful moment of any presentation is the one minute before your stage entrance. Use the tactic of elite athletes by visualizing a positive outcome and using deep belly breathing to reduce stress and build confidence.

Find a Friend: Prior to your public speaking on stage introduce yourself to a few members of the audience in the front row. During your talk look these people in the eye to ease your nerves and connect with your audience.

Engage the Audience: Creating a monologue presentation puts the entire task of informing and entertaining the audience on you. Make your talk a two-way interaction with questions and participation to reduce boredom and speak with ease. Having the group involved also gives you time to reorganize your thoughts if things are going off track.

Make public speaking part of your marketing function and boost your business success. Your fears will evaporate over time and you will wonder why you didn't start sooner.

Chapter 56 - Be the One

> *"Most of the important things in the world have been accomplished by people who have kept on trying when there seemed to be no hope at all."*
>
> — Dale Carnegie

Never passively wait for the right time or moment to move forward. The time is now. You have a winner inside of you that is waiting to break free. What you are now does not define the true person you will become. You are not an animal that is subject to instinct and seasons for survival. You are human. You have the power to change your circumstances radically. You can change the car you're driving now to the car of your dreams. You can realize your goal of owning that dream home. You can travel to the places you've always dreamed of.

The only thing stopping you is YOU. It's time to write a new chapter in the book of your life. What is life if you never succeed at the things you desire? These rules apply to every area of your life. Don't believe the lie that you'll never have a great relationship, be a great parent, or reach your health goals. Choose right now to make this your reality. Stop spending hundreds of dollars on gossip magazines so that you can read someone else's story! Now is your story! BE THE ONE.

A New Season a New Reason

On the road to success, the challenge will be to keep going when things aren't going your way. You must continually revisit your list of goals. Save your old goals for comparison – to see how far you've com. Your goals should push you to the edge where you are a little outside your comfort zone. Each season in your life should give you a new reason to make new goals. Don't stop when you've just reached one of them. Go on until you've reached it all!

Here are some practical ways to keep you motivated for the game every day:

Condition your mind.

Train yourself to think positive thoughts.

Condition your body.

It takes physical energy to take action.

Avoid negative people.

Don't take anything that they say seriously.

Always remain flexible.

No plan should be cast in concrete.

Act with a higher purpose.

If it doesn't serve your goal, it's wasted effort.

Take responsibility for your own results.

Don't credit luck, good or bad.

Stretch past your limits on a daily basis.

That's how you grow and evolve.

Don't wait for perfection; do it now!

Perfection's the enemy of good enough.

Hang around self-motivated people.

The positive energy will rub off on you.

I know this stuff works from own my personal experience. After I came up with this list, I began to read the list to myself at the beginning of each workday. For an entire week, I made a point of referring back to them every time I had a lull in my work schedule. By the end of the week, they were influencing my thinking so much that I felt like a new person.

Note: While I was energizing myself in this way, I was propelled to do something that I'd been putting off for years. A phone call and two emails later and I had resold the rights to one of my out-of-print books. I'll now end up with about $10,000 in additional royalties for a writing I did nearly five years ago — all because I motivated myself to do a little extra.

I'll bet there are some calls that you could make — but aren't — or connections you could develop — but aren't, all for the lack of a little extra motivation. If you'll take this list seriously, and make living it into part of your daily routine, I can practically guarantee that you'll quickly push your career — and your ability to sell — up to the next level.

Self-motivation is the ultimate root of success. Especially in sales.

Chapter 57 - Take Responsibility for your Sale

> *"Never be satisfied with what you achieve, because it all pales in comparison with what you are capable of doing in the future."*
> - Rabbi Nochem Kaplan

I remember selling a property that I had purchased to resell. I had searched for an agent in the area who had sold homes recently. The agent told me he would do a huge marketing plan and get buyers to look at my home. He promised me he could sell it quickly.

Once the contract was signed, I waited and waited for buyers to come and look at my property. Six months later I was pretty frustrated. I contacted the agent and asked what was going on. He said they were doing the best they could and that eventually someone would come along and buy it. I thought, "It's been six months and I haven't had any action other than my nosey neighbors looking at this house. So I fired the agent and found someone else to do the task of marketing and selling my home. This agent was a referral from a friend. Three months later, there I was, still with no action on selling the property.

I had to come up with a new strategy, so I fired that agent as well. I started attending networking events and learning about real estate. I realized that I had been pricing myself out of the market for the area that I was in. I immediately invested in an appraisal that guided me to the price that was right for my property. Two supposedly top real estate agents had failed to do this simple thing.

Next, I came up with a marketing plan. I hit the streets and passed out flyers and advertising all around the area. I started to get calls all day.

Some prospects didn't qualify but I was just happy to be getting some action on the property. Eventually someone called who loved the home and qualified for it as well. I sold that property within the first 60 days!

Sometimes we put our trust in people to do what we need to do ourselves. We must always be trying to educate ourselves on whatever type of industry we want to embark upon and not leave it up to chance. If I had had a deadline to sell the house or go into foreclosure I couldn't hold the agents responsible. I had to be accountable for my sale ultimately. I was so excited about what had happened in that deal I sold my next house in 30 days and got a contract the first day!

Chapter 58 - Fight for your Profit First

> *"Great things are not done by impulse, but by a series of small things brought together."*
>
> - Vincent Van Gogh

Never cave in when your customer tells you they got a lower rate somewhere else. This is your time to sell. Take a deep breath - this can get interesting! Listen even more intently to your prospect. Get a good sense of what the competition has offered them and look for the weak areas. If you sense your customer starts to doubt something the other guy said, go in for the kill. If you have a solution to their problem and you can create value, price will become less of an issue. You must be fully educated on all the features and benefits of your product in order to show this to your prospect.

I recommend rebutting at least three times before settling with a lower offering. Don't get nervous or act out of fear, just listen to your prospect. When they're done, just shake your head in a positive manner and let them know you plan on solving their problem, once you ask a few questions. You must ask questions to take control and find a solution that creates more value or uncovers another need.

Most prospects are busy and don't really have the time to research products completely. Whoever makes them feel they are saving money or getting the best deal wins. You have to make sure your prospect is comparing apples to apples and not lemons. Many companies throw out low ball offers just to get the prospects' attention. I call these non-salesmen, because they prey on prospects by luring them in with offers that are not the bottom line. They usually add the real price in once the customer signs the deal, leaving the customer to find out the truth when it's too late.

I once worked with a car dealership that advertised a really nice car in the newspaper and even parked it in front of the dealership to lure customers in. Once the customer got on the lot they realized the car didn't have any of the features that they wanted. The dealership would usually bump the customers price range up subconsciously by adding the things that the customer wanted item by item until the prospect was right where they needed to be.

You must thoroughly understand your product line and know want you can and can't do. And as long as its ethical, it's your job to make a profit, it's the customer's job to take as much away from you as possible. It's also your job to learn what your competition is doing and why they are able to make such an offer. This will give you the ability to be specific with your prospect with what you know about the deficiencies of your competition.

You should also always be looking for ways to add more value in your service, and be looking for ways to stand out over your competition. I've been in situations where the competition was giving away free products and I didn't, but still walked away with the deal in hand.

Of course, if at the end of the conversation you find that you're just not able to offer a product to a customer at a rate that fits their budget, you'll still have the upper hand if you leave your information and walk away. Follow up with them later. Count the time you spent with them as experience. You need customers like that to help you get stronger in your presentation. Pat yourself on the back knowing that you offered something you knew you could stand behind. Stand your ground. By bringing value to this customer you are also making an investment in the long term value of your industry. The marketplace wants value, and the more you offer it, you'll always close deals and have prospects calling you for your service.

You're talking to a customer and after you present your product, service or solution, she asks, "What discount can I get?" or "What can you do about the price?" Think before you speak otherwise this innocent-sounding question will cost you money right off your bottom line. While it's tempting to offer a discount or better price resist the desire to do so. Here's why:

First, just because someone asks you for a better price, does not mean they expect to get it. Some people ask for a discount because they have been told to. They are often uncomfortable doing this and will seldom press the issue. However, professional buyers and key decision-makers know that many sellers will drop their price at the first sign of resistance so they ask everyone for a discount-and they can be aggressive in their approach. Plus, experienced negotiators lose respect for people who drop their price too quickly. Standing your ground and refusing to cave in right away is also a show of strength and executives respect this type of behavior.

Second, when you drop your price too quickly, you teach your customer to repeat that behavior in future transactions. Remember, everything you do now affects your customer's behavior toward you in the future. When I first started my private practice, I gave a client a discount on a package of services. The next time he contacted, he demanded that same discount which put me in a somewhat precarious position-did I give the same discount or risk losing the sale? A business executive once told me that she knew which of her suppliers she could browbeat into giving her a better price and she always took advantage of that perceived weakness.

So, what is the best way to respond to a request for a discount or better price?

Professional negotiators will tell you not to flinch. A flinch is a visible reaction to a request or demand and goes something like this, "You want a discount? Even though we have been working together for four years and you know our services will help you get better results you still want a discount?" When coupled with the right facial expressions and body language, this technique is extremely effective. However, I have found that most people are extremely uncomfortable using this approach and even I find it difficult to apply on a consistent basis.

An effective way to respond to a request for a better price is to ask, "What did you have in mind?" or "What were you looking for?" When you asked one of these questions, you get the other person to tell you how much of a discount they want. In many cases, their expectation will be less than you are prepared to give which means you will increase the size of the sale and save money at the same time - a double win. One word of caution here; an experienced negotiator will say, "Well, I want a better price than this" which means you need to be prepared to ask the question a couple of times.

This also applies to email correspondence. Many people will ask their sales person for a discount via email which makes it next to impossible to use some of the standard negotiating techniques. Before you respond by offering a better price, take the time to properly craft your email. Here is what you can say, "We might be able to do something for you. What did you have in mind?" The key is to give the indication that you have flexibility without committing to something you might regret later.

This sounds like an easy technique to use but it's not. You have to train yourself to listen for your customer's question and be prepared to respond with your own. I hate to admit it but I have fallen for this question because I wasn't expecting it. In one situation, an existing client asked me for a package price on some bundled services. Instead of responding by asking what price he was looking for, I automatically offered a small discount. I kicked myself afterwards because I felt that I should have known better.

It is essential to listen carefully to what your prospect says and to think before you speak. It is also critical to practice asking your question until it becomes second-nature so you can respond quickly when a prospect asks for a discount or better price.

Chapter 59 - Take Control

> *"An achievement is a bondage. It obliges one to a higher achievement."*
> -Albert Camus

Always fully present your product or service before stating a price. This allows you to build value and help the customer understand clearly what you are offering. Another reason not to give the price first is because your customer may only be numbers shopping. If you quote a price before effectively communicating your value, you could price yourself out of the game.

Every time you begin a presentation, make sure there are no loud, distracting background noises. Ask some qualifying questions that relate to your service, but not too many, or you may make them nervous. Sometimes a prospect wants me to rush through a presentation. I always tell them that if I don't inform them completely, I'll be doing them a disservice.

From the moment you first interact with a customer you must be in total control. You must tell the customer what to do and think. The hard part is doing this in a way that is unnoticeable. You can't just tell the customer to do something. You have to politely ask in a non-offensive way. If you don't have control from beginning to end it may be difficult to close the deal.

It is imperative that your control is established in the beginning of your sales pitch. I remember once I went with another salesman to a demonstration and the customer would be doing something in a totally different room. I would have to explain to them the importance of taking control from the beginning. If the customer isn't listening to your pitch, then you are wasting your time. Don't let the customer do other activities during your pitch. Make sure and keep them locked in throughout your pitch.

When you are in a customer's home make sure you get the customer involved in your pitch. Whether it's getting them to your product or asking them questions to keep their attention, it is important to not lose the interest of the customer. I always say a good salesman is like an entertainer. If you are putting on a good pitch people will be focused on you through your whole sales pitch without distraction.

There will always be uncontrollable factors such as unexpected house guests or unforeseen phone calls. The best thing for a salesman to do in these situations is to wait politely for them to finish before continuing your pitch. If possible get the house guest involved in your sales pitch as well. This may help you avoid third party objection.

The key to keeping control is keeping the customer involved. If the customer becomes bored you will lose control fast. Try to avoid repeating yourself. Being redundant is a quick way to lose a customers interest. Keep them on the edge of their seat with new information throughout your pitch.

Relative stories are always a good way to keep control of the customer. Make sure the story is something they can relate to. When I was selling vacuums I would tell the customer a story of a lady who didn't invest in the vacuum, then her carpet was destroyed by the dirt. She had to pay 3 times as much as the Kirby investment to get her carpet replaced.

People generally like hearing stories. Even back when we were little and wanted our parents to read us a bedtime story. If your story relates to the person in some form it will keep them interested. As long as you have their interest you can keep control. Remember a good salesman must maintain control throughout his sales pitch in order to solidify a sale.

Chapter 60 – Keep Your Focus

> *"High achievement always takes place in the framework of high expectation."*
>
> - Jack Kinder

Any successful person will tell you that your biggest challenge is to stay focused on your goal. Your environment and the people in it will always tell you success is impossible. Whether it's the economy's fault, the president's fault, or anyone and everything's fault, they refuse to take personal responsibility. This is the way they tolerate their own lack of ambition.

Start **today** to blame-proof your life. Take responsibility for where **you** are. Forget everyone else's excuses. It's impossible for you to change others, so stick with changing yourself. Some people focus on their race or their gender as an excuse. They fail to admit that many people facing greater challenges than they do have been tremendously successful. Certain people actually feel better when they blame someone else. It lets them take the focus off of their own failures.

I have some good news for you – no matter what your background or circumstances are, you have the opportunity to live your dreams. For starters, you live in America. America is all about opportunity. Even those who are extremely disadvantaged can improve their quality of life by leaps and bounds just by keeping their eyes open and believing in their dreams.

Consider someone who comes to America from a place where he was only able to make $30 a month. He realizes that opportunity is right here, and he determines to reach out and grab it. He sees that he could easily make the $30 he made each month in one hour here. Thousands of people risk their lives everyday to get here and those that make it understand that to be successful, they must work. Americans have access to education and a wide variety of support systems that are not as available in other countries. Everything is readily available for the ones that are ready to take the challenge.

Are you ready? So what if you fail, you can start again! I've learned that failure is a part of success. If you don't fail, you can't be successful. You only really fail if you quit and never get up again. There have been many, many times when I wanted to give up or give in, but I chose to keep going. As I went forward, I realized that the solution to my problem was getting closer. My fears got smaller, my negative thinking got smaller, and then something miraculous happened - my goal had gotten closer!

Don't let others sabotage your chances of living your dreams. As long as you have an opportunity and are ready you will turn your dreams into reality. In any market there will be winners and losers. What you must do is to increase your odds of being the winner. Ask yourself if you are you maximizing all the opportunities that you've had. Look for the opportunities others are missing. This is when you can swoop in like an eagle and soar to the highest mountain a winner.

Beginning vs End

Don't be afraid to be a beginner. To get anywhere, you have to begin. You must learn some new things and adapt to your surrounding. A baby must crawl before he can walk. He must learn how to talk. He must learn how to ride a bike. He has to learn all these things through trial and error.

When we become adults, we forget that we've made it this far in life by adapting to new circumstances and challenges every day. We forget that mistakes are inevitable, and we're discouraged and frustrated when we make them. But the miracle of all of this is that we can change and improve ourselves in small steps every day. We can be better next year that we are this year.

It's never too late to make a radical change. It could happen at any moment. "I want to change my career." "I want a higher income." These are things we can resolve to do and begin to accomplish at any moment. Where you're living now doesn't determine where you will live next year. Your income now doesn't have to be your income next year. Don't ever look at the present to determine your future. I always continue to dream of how far I can go. When I was driving a car that needed the radiator filled with water every 10 miles to avoid embarrassing smoke, I never stopped dreaming of my "dream car." When I was living in a one-bedroom apartment, I still dreamed of having an office in a new home. As your dreams grow, so will your determination to obtain them. Your main obstacle is fear of failure – and even fear of success!

This doesn't mean you should fool yourself into thinking that these things will magically happen. It will usually require guts and hard work. For things to change from the way that they are now you have to change. If you don't successfully apply action to your decisions, you will certainly be doing the same things next year as you are this year.

You're Fired!

In today's highly competitive world of business, no company can afford to have a weak link. Non-productive employees waste time on the job and cost their employers profit. The employer wants to be able to provide an opportunity to someone who is willing to do the job to the best of their ability. Companies have fired thousands of employees over the years simply because the marketplace has gotten more fierce. Companies must make many critical decisions throughout the day just in order to survive. With growing competition you must be looking for ways to stand out from those that are about to be fired.

In the global economy today, you shouldn't even see yourself a an employee. You should see yourself as a skilled professional. A skilled professional takes the initiative to look for ways to improve their skills and learn new skills. They are not waiting for the pink slips to come because they know that even if they are laid off, their skills make them valuable. On the other hand, an employer would be reluctant to let them go, because they are the ones bringing value to the company.

Usually, the first departments to go in a layoff are the non-sales departments. Sales is usually the last because they are the ones who bring in the revenue. A company will always look for the weakest link that are just running up the company tab. Employees like these are usually more concerned about the weekend than their job. Many companies are now outsourcing their work overseas or to domestic virtual assistants who work harder, cost less, and are available on an as-needed basis. Don't fool yourself – there is a growing workforce that is more than willing to take your job and do it better for less.

Don't be surprised when you see more and more companies moving their operations overseas. Many factors go into a company's bottom line calculation. They must hire CPAs and accountants to track payroll and pay taxes. They need lawyers to keep them in compliance with ordinances and regulations. When a companies salaried employers are wasting time and demanding more, it makes sense that non-salaried, harder workers could solve a lot of problems and make the company more profitable.

Don't become a statistic. Be the one who becomes proactive and in control. Don't look for a company to take care of you, take care of yourself by making yourself more valuable by learning more skills. If you love your job, then do more than what you are paid to do – don't just do the minimum and watch the clock to see how long you can ride it out at the company's expense. Put yourself in the position to fire your company if you decide you want a change, not the other way around!

The Sellionaire™

I would like to thank you for reviewing The Sellionaire. I hope the information that I've provided has helped inspire you to reach your ultimate goals. In the journey to find your destiny there are many people along the way that will help you put together life's puzzle.

My only hope is that I've made a small deposit into your life that will help create something that you will remember and reward you for generations to come.

Thank you

The Sellionaire

For product orders, seminars schedules, or corporate speaking inquiries, please contact:

For Information:
Antonio Clyde Smith International
925 Main St. Ste 50-71
Stone Mountain, Ga 30083
678-476-3715
770-234-5849 fax
www.thesellionaire.com

Sign up for FREE weekly e-zine
info@thesellionaire.com

Antonio Clyde Smith has been in sales since the age of twelve. Today, a sales trainer and business strategist, Tony conducts seminars throughout the United States, teaching, training, and motivating audiences. His diverse background includes a lifestyle mission statement that focuses on vision, integrity, and diligence. The founder of Antonio Clyde Smith International, an author, and the creator of several inspirational CDs and DVDs, Tony is committed to bringing out the winner in everyone.